EXPRESS

ENGLISH

Beginnings 2
Beginning Student Book

LINDA A. FERREIRA

NEWBURY HOUSE PUBLISHERS, INC.

Library of Congress Cataloging in Publication Data

Ferreira, Linda A.
  Express English/Beginnings 2

  (Express English series)
  1. English language—Text-books for foreign speakers.
I. Title. II. Series: Ferreira, Linda A. Express
English series.
PE1128.F4268 1985   428.2′4   85-13801
ISBN 0-88377-304-X

Project editor/James W. Brown
Design and production/Designworks, Inc.
Illustrators/Margie Frem/Peter Zafris/Diana Maloney
Photo research/Olivia Gould/Janice Miller/Leslie Berriman

NEWBURY HOUSE PUBLISHERS, INC.

Language Science
Language Teaching
Language Learning

ROWLEY, MASSACHUSETTS 01969
ROWLEY ● LONDON ● TOKYO

Credits

The author wishes to thank the following people and organizations for the photographs appearing throughout the book:

Walt Disney Productions: 9; Bruce AF Polsky: 16, 45, 53, 61, 69; Smithsonian Institution: 37; Volkswagen of America: 48; Ford Division/Public Relations: 48; Department of Commerce/NOAA/National Geophysical Data Center: 57; Georgina Sculco: 72; Taurus Photos, Inc. S. Berkowitz: 73; © Universal Pictures: 73; Photo courtesy of San Diego Convention and Visitors Bureau: 73.

Copyright © 1985 by Newbury House Publishers, Inc. All rights reserved. No part of this book may be reproduced or transmitted in any form or by any means, electronic or mechanical, including photocopying, recording, or by any information storage and retrieval system, without permission in writing from the Publisher.

First printing: October 1985
Printed in the U.S.A.   5 4 3 2

Contents

Scenes	Language	Themes
19 Alex and Willy held onto the rope. Ken was hanging from the other end. *74, 75*	*Practice* Integration *76*	*Expression* 1 Make an exchange 2 Discuss alternatives *77*
20 Everyone was safe in the police helicopter. Ana had to think about the future. *78, 79*	*Transfer* Entertainment *80*	*Hearabout/Speakabout* Talk about advantages and disadvantages *81*

Beginnings 2

Beginning Student Book

LANDSLIDE!

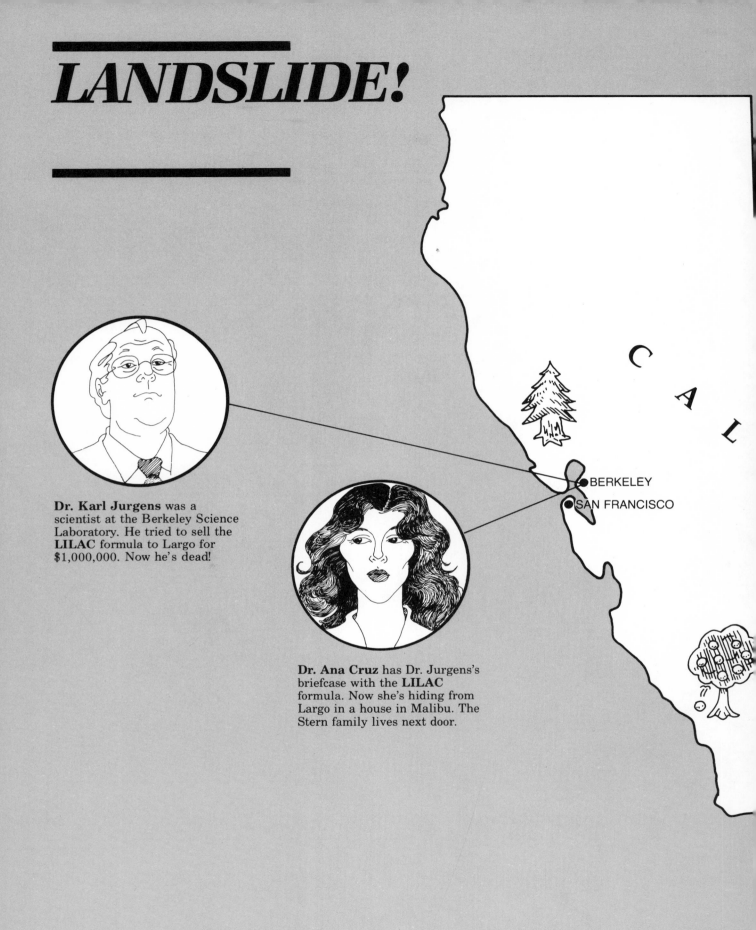

Dr. Karl Jurgens was a scientist at the Berkeley Science Laboratory. He tried to sell the **LILAC** formula to Largo for $1,000,000. Now he's dead!

Dr. Ana Cruz has Dr. Jurgens's briefcase with the **LILAC** formula. Now she's hiding from Largo in a house in Malibu. The Stern family lives next door.

BERKELEY

SAN FRANCISCO

C A L

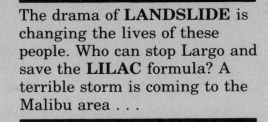

The drama of **LANDSLIDE** is changing the lives of these people. Who can stop Largo and save the **LILAC** formula? A terrible storm is coming to the Malibu area . . .

Ken Matthews, a U.S. agent, can save Ana and the **LILAC** formula. But is there time? Largo is looking for Ana too. Ken has to find Ana first.

Largo is a dangerous terrorist. He followed Ana from Berkeley to Malibu. Largo needs the **LILAC** formula. He might hurt Ana.

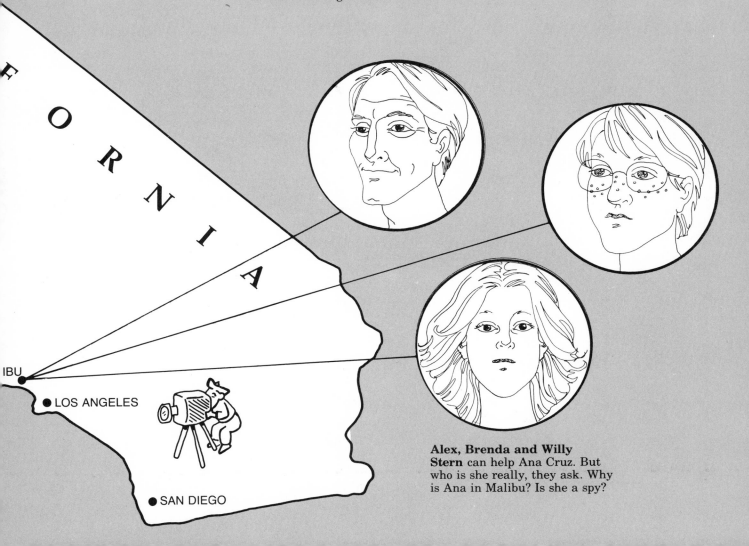

Alex, Brenda and Willy Stern can help Ana Cruz. But who is she really, they ask. Why is Ana in Malibu? Is she a spy?

Ken is picking up the telephone. He's going to call Ana.

*Largo's leaving.
I'm going to follow him.
Hide the formula.*

Scene One

Ken Matthews was next to the telephone booths in the airport terminal. He picked up the telephone and dialed.

On the beach, Ana said good-bye to Willy. She walked up the wooden steps to the lower deck. She looked down. There were big rocks in the ocean below. Then she walked up to the house. The telephone rang.

ANA Hello?
KEN Ana? It's Ken. I'm in Los Angeles.
ANA Thank God you're here, Ken. Largo called me in San Francisco. He's looking for me and the LILAC formula.
KEN Yes, I know. He was on my plane to Los Angeles.
ANA What? Largo here, in Los Angeles?
KEN Listen, Ana. Hide the LILAC formula. Put it in a safe place.
ANA But what about Largo? Is he going to come here?
KEN Don't worry, Ana. Oh . . . Largo's leaving the terminal. I'm going to follow him. Hide the formula, Ana.

Questions

1 Who made the telephone call?
2 What did Ana see in the ocean below?
3 Who has the LILAC formula?
4 Where is Largo going?
5 Who's following Largo?

Scene Two

Ken ran over to the rental car counter. He took his identification card from his pocket and showed the ID to the clerk.

KEN Where did that man go? What kind of car does he have?

CLERK He rented a Buick, a tan one. And he asked about Malibu. I gave him maps.

KEN Quick, give me keys to a car. What else did he say?

CLERK I told him about a motel. The Surfer Motel on Ocean Beach Drive.

KEN Thanks. Where's the car?

CLERK It's the blue Ford. It's in the parking lot to the right of the terminal. Hey, who's going to pay for the car? Hey, wait, mister. You get a free ticket to Disneyland with the car . . .

Questions

1 Where did Ken go?
2 What was in his pocket?
3 Which car was Largo's?
4 Where's the Surfer Motel?
5 Where's the blue Ford?

Speechwork

1 He's *going to* call Ana. [gənə]
2 I'm *going to* follow her. [gənə]

GOING TO Future

Is	Ken / Ana	going to follow Largo?	Yes, he is. / No, she isn't.

Tomorrow is Saturday.	I'm not / She isn't / We aren't	going to get up early.

I'm going
we're going
you're going + *to* + Verb
he's going
they're going

A **Tell about the story.**

1 Ken picks up the telephone. Who is he going to call?
He's going to call Ana.
2 Ana says good-bye to Willy. Where is she going to go?
3 Largo is at the rental car counter. What is he going to do?

● **What do you think is going to happen?**

1 Willy is putting on his bathing suit.
He's going to go for a swim.
2 Brenda is opening the refrigerator door.
3 Alex is putting a piece of paper into the typewriter.
4 Willy and Brenda are looking at the TV Guide.
5 Brenda is driving to Burger Queen.
6 Ana is looking for the shampoo.
7 Alex and Willy are putting clothes into the washing machine.
8 Willy is opening his math book.

B **Tell about things you have to do. What are you going to do today? This week? This month?**

Bills to pay.

Clothes to pick up.

Household chores to do.

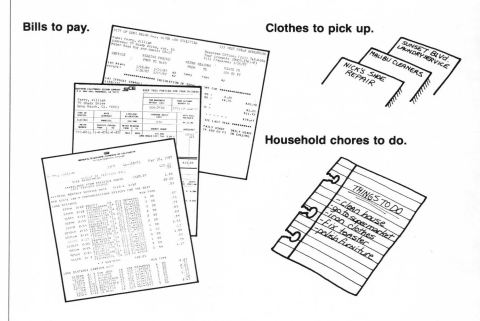

C **Brenda doesn't have school on Saturday. It's her free day.**

Every Saturday, Brenda gets up at ten. She goes to the beach with her friends. Later in the afternoon, they have a picnic on the beach. On Saturday night, Brenda goes to a movie or to a disco.

● **Ask about Brenda's free day, like this:**

Is Brenda going to get up at eight?
No, she isn't. She's going to get up at ten.

● **Ask about *your* free day, like this:**

Are you going to	get up early see a movie eat out play sports study English	?

I'm (not) going to get up at _____ .

1 *Make arrangements*

Largo drove to the Surfer Motel. He parked the car, got out, and went into the motel office. Largo is talking to the motel manager.
Listen to the conversation. Listen again and write the missing words.

MANAGER May I help you, sir?
LARGO I want a _____, please. A _____ room.
MANAGER How long are you _____ _____ stay?
LARGO Two or _____ days.
MANAGER The room is $_____ a day. Are you _____ _____ pay with cash or a credit card?
LARGO Cash. And I want a room in _____ _____. A quiet one.
MANAGER Number 23. Here's the _____. You can park your car _____ _____.
LARGO Fine. And I _____ want any visitors.
MANAGER Yes, sir.

Role Play: Choose one of these situations. Make arrangements to stay at the Surfer Motel. You are traveling. . .

1 with a friend and you want to stay for two days.
2 with your family and you want to stay for a week.
3 alone and you want to stay for four or five days.

2 *Talk about calendar dates*

Brenda was sixteen years old last month. Her birthday is on December third.

BRENDA When's your birthday, Maria?
MARIA This month. My birthday's on January 20th.
BRENDA Really? Willy's birthday is on January 22nd.

● **When's *your* birthday?**

It's *in* January.
It's *on* January 20th.

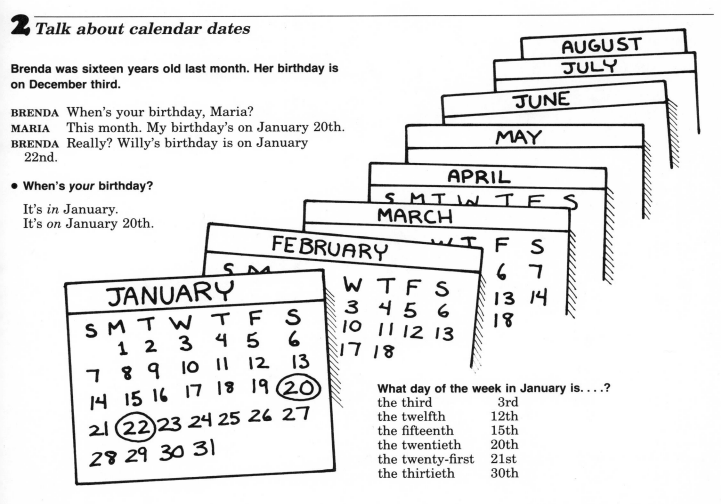

What day of the week in January is. . . .?
the third   3rd
the twelfth   12th
the fifteenth   15th
the twentieth   20th
the twenty-first   21st
the thirtieth   30th

The seashell is on the table. Ana is going to put the LILAC formula inside the shell.

The shell looks great now. Back in a minute.

Scene One

📷 Slowly, Ana put down the telephone. The briefcase was on the couch. She opened it and took out a piece of paper. Carefully, she folded the paper. Then Ana washed the shell and dried it with a clean cloth. With a knife, she pushed the folded paper into the shell. Ana put the shell on the table and went into the bathroom.

There was a knock at the door. Willy ran into the room.

WILLY Ana, Ana, where are you?

ANA I'm in the shower, Willy.

WILLY C'mon. Get dressed. Dad wants you to come over for dinner. Hey, you cleaned my shell. Ana, I want to put the shell in my room.

ANA No, Willy . . . Wait for me!

WILLY Wow! The shell looks great now. Back in a minute.

ANA Willy? Willy? Are you there?

Questions

1 What was on the couch?
2 Did Ana hide the LILAC formula? Where?
3 Who knocked on the door?
4 Who's in the bathroom?
5 Is Willy going to wait for Ana?

Scene Two

📼 Brenda took the chicken out of the oven. On the deck, Alex put the chairs around the table. When Ana and Willy arrived, Alex served dinner. Later, he put water on the stove for coffee.

ANA   The chicken was really nice, Alex. Thank you for inviting me.

WILLY   Yeah, and there's ice cream too.

ALEX   I'm sorry about the dinner. We don't cook much.

ANA   Oh, it was fine. I really enjoyed it, but it's late. I have to leave now.

ALEX   Where are you from, Ana?

ANA   Uh . . . San Francisco.

BRENDA   What do you do there?

ANA   Uh . . . I'm a . . . uh . . . a secretary. For . . . uh . . . a computer company.

ALEX   Are you going to stay in Malibu?

ANA   Oh . . . uh . . . I don't know.

BRENDA   Don't you know? Is that your house? How come you don't live there all the time?

ALEX   Brenda, don't ask so many questions. It's not polite. Willy, Brenda. You two clean up. Ana, it's dark. I'm going to walk you home.

WILLY   C'mon, Brenda. Let's have some ice cream.

Questions

1 What's for dinner?
2 Is Ana a secretary?
3 Does Brenda like Ana?
4 Who's going to walk Ana to her house?
5 What are Willy and Brenda going to eat?

Speechwork

1 When are you *going to* leave? [gənə]

2 Where are you *going to* stay? [gənə]

3 Who are you *going to* visit? [gənə]

Vacations

What do you enjoy doing on your vacation?

A trip . . .	to the mountains	to the beach	to the city
accommodations	a small cabin with no electricity no hot water	a quiet guest house with a fish restaurant a white sandy beach	an expensive hotel with TV and air-conditioning bars and restaurants
activities	fishing hiking reading	swimming sailing surfing	shopping sightseeing eating out
transportation	by foot by horseback	by bicycle by boat	by taxi by bus

A Plan your vacation.

1 Which trip are you going to take?
2 Where are you going to stay?
3 How long are you going to visit?
4 Who's going to go with you?
5 How are you going to get around?

B Plan your activities.

1 Are you going to | get up early / stay out late | ?

2 What are you going to do all day?

I	(don't) enjoy love/hate (don't) like	hiking. sailing. shopping.

C What clothes are you going to take?

bluejeans	bathing suit	socks
T-shirts	shorts	boots
sweater	pajamas	running shoes
dress	underwear	raincoat
suit	evening dress	walking shoes

Disneyland— A Guided Tour

© Walt Disney Productions

Good morning, everyone. I'm going to take you through the magical lands of Disneyland.

We're going to visit **Adventureland** and see wild animals on our boat trip through the jungle. We're going to climb to the top of Swiss Family Treehouse.

In **Frontierland** we're going to see America's Old West and travel through the Rivers of America. Mom and Dad can rest. I'm going to take the children to Tom Sawyer's Island.

In our trip through **Fantasyland,** we're going to walk through the magic castle and meet Mickey Mouse and Donald Duck. And you're going to take a photograph with Mickey to show friends back home.

From October through February, **Disneyland** is open from ten A.M. to six P.M., Wednesday through Friday, and from ten A.M. to seven P.M. Saturday and Sunday.

Thinkabout

	True	False
1 You travel through Adventureland by boat.	✓	
2 You can see Mickey Mouse in Frontierland.		
3 In December, Disneyland is usually open from ten to seven on Wednesday and Thursday.		
4 Children pay $5.00 for the guided tour.		

Hotels and Motels in the Disneyland Area

Featured are over ten thousand rooms in over one hundred hotels and motels, with accommodations from deluxe to economy. For information and reservations, write the

Anaheim Area Visitor & Convention Bureau, P.O. Box 4270, Anaheim, CA 92803.

Complete this letter. Ask for information about *your* vacation.

_____
(your street)

_____
(your city)

_____
(today's date)

Dear Sir,

I'm going to take my family to Disneyland in _____. We need a room for _____ people. We're going to stay for _____ days. The dates are _____ to _____.

Please send me information about accommodations. We want to spend about $_____ a night for a room.

Yours truly,

_____

Quietly, Ken Matthews got out of his car. Largo's tan Buick was parked in front of room 23.

> Drop the gun.
> Or you die,
> right now.

Scene One

🔊 Largo watched from the window of his room at the Surfer Motel. He took out his gun. A tall man got out of a blue Ford. Ken moved quickly.

Ken stood in front of Largo's door. He opened his coat and pulled out his gun. Ken pushed against the door and jumped into the room. It was empty. Largo was behind him.

LARGO	Drop the gun. Now!
KEN	Largo, is that you?
LARGO	Stop the talk. Drop the gun. Or you die, right now.
KEN	Okay, okay, Largo.
LARGO	Over there, next to that chair. Move.
KEN	I'm going. I'm going. Take it easy.
LARGO	Sit down. Hands behind your back. I'm tying you up. Then I'm going to find out who you are.

Questions

1 Who was in the blue Ford?
2 Where did Largo park his car?
3 Who had a gun?
4 Was the room empty?
5 Did Largo know Ken's name?

Scene Two

Largo opened the curtains. It was a sunny morning in southern California. When the sun hit his face, Ken woke up. There were bruises on Ken's face.

In one hand, Largo held Ken's identification card. In his other hand, he had a gun.

LARGO Good morning, Mr. Matthews. So, you're a U.S. agent. Are you ready to talk this morning?

KEN Talk about what? I don't know anything.

LARGO Yes, you do, Mr. Matthews. Tell me, why did you follow me?

KEN Don't you remember? You went through that red traffic light. You know, the one on the corner.

LARGO I'm not laughing, Mr. Matthews. Don't tell me your bad jokes. I want an answer. Why did you follow me?

KEN You're wasting your time. I'm not going to tell you.

LARGO I have time, Mr. Matthews. Lots of time. I can wait. I'm a very patient man.

You're wasting your time. I'm not going to tell you.

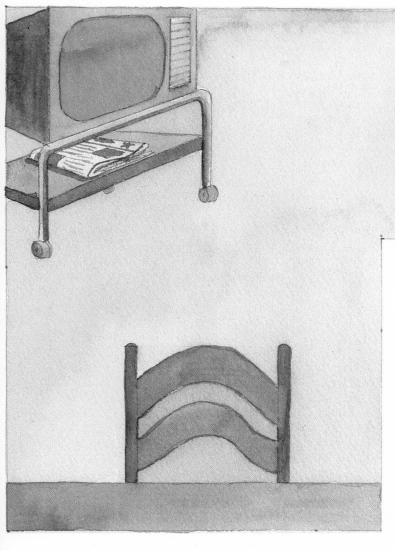

Questions

1 Why did Ken wake up?
2 Did Largo hurt Ken?
3 How did Largo know Ken's name?
4 What was Ken's joke about?
5 Who is a patient man?

Speechwork

1 a blue Ford

2 a traffic light

3 a red traffic light

Adjectives and Adverbs

Alex writes wonderful stories.	He	writes well.
		is a good writer.

Largo has long black hair. He's wearing an old brown suit.

Alex likes to drive 80 miles an hour.	He	is a fast driver.
		doesn't drive slowly.

Adjectives		Adverbs
slow	+ <u>ly</u> →	slow<u>ly</u>
easy		easi<u>ly</u>
but		
good		well
fast	→	fast
hard		hard

A Tell about Alex. Practice adjectives and adverbs.

1 good/well
  He writes *well.*
  He's a *good* writer.
2 bad/badly
  He's a _____ cook.
  He cooks _____.
3 heavy/heavily
  He smokes _____.
  He's a _____ smoker.
4 neat/neatly
  He's a _____ dresser.
  He dresses _____.

● Make questions and ask each other:

1 run fast
  Do you run fast?
  Are you a fast runner?
2 sing well
3 work hard
4 write carefully
5 think quickly
6 walk slowly

B Largo is a dangerous terrorist. The police want to catch him. Tell about Largo.

WANTED!
INTERNATIONAL TERRORIST—LARGO

The police are looking for this man. Largo is six feet tall and weighs 220 pounds. He has long black hair and a thick black mustache. His eyes are dark brown. Largo is a violent man. Call the police immediately when you see him.

1 He has (a, black, thick) mustache.
  He has a thick black mustache.
2 He is wearing (brown, an, old) suit.
3 He has (brown, dark) eyes.
4 He is driving (large, tan, a) Buick.
5 He has (black, long) hair.

a(n) my	old large dark	green American	car

C Complete these statements about people in the story. Use the adverbs in the chart.

Adverbs—opposites	
carefully	carelessly
early	late
loudly	softly
politely	rudely
slowly	fast
well	badly

1 Brenda is a loud talker. She talks _____ on the telephone. She doesn't speak _____.
2 Willy gets A's in school. He does his homework _____. Brenda isn't careful. She does her work _____.
3 Brenda doesn't get up _____. She likes to sleep _____.
4 Alex likes to drive 80 miles an hour. He drives _____. He doesn't like to drive _____.
5 Largo doesn't say "Please." He speaks _____. He doesn't greet people _____.
6 Maria gets good grades in languages but not in science. Maria does _____ in French, but she does _____ in chemistry.

1 *Give strong opinions*

Brenda saw two movies last week. Maria is thinking of going to see a movie tonight.
Listen to the conversation. Listen again and write the missing words.

MARIA   Well, how was the movie? Did you like *Tarzan*?
BRENDA Oh, *that* movie! It was _____. The acting was lousy. I left _____. The action was too _____.
MARIA   Didn't you _____ it at all?
BRENDA No, it was pretty _____.
MARIA   What _____ the new Indiana Jones one?
BRENDA Oh, that was a _____ movie. I loved it. The story moved very _____ and the characters were interesting.
MARIA   I guess you really _____ the movie.
BRENDA Yeah, it was great.

Role Play: Ask about movies, books or TV programs you know about.

Start with: How was the *book*? Did you like _____?

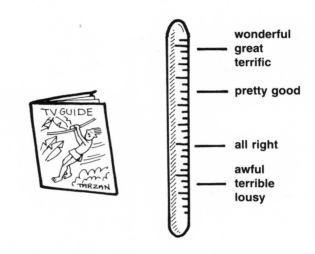

wonderful
great
terrific

pretty good

all right

awful
terrible
lousy

2 *Describe a person*

Brenda is walking along the beach. She is looking for her father. Brenda asks a man about her father.

BRENDA Excuse me. I'm looking for my father.
MAN   What does he look like?
BRENDA Well, he's tall and he has straight brown hair. He's wearing a red T-shirt and yellow shorts.
MAN   Is that your father over there, near those rocks?
BRENDA Yeah, that's him. Thanks.

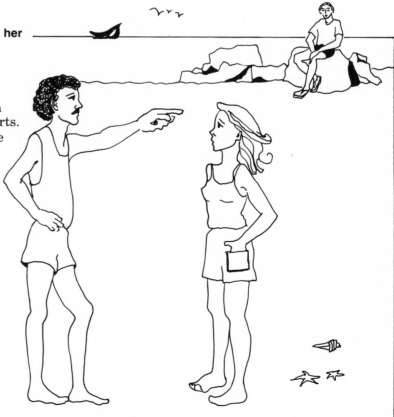

● Ask each other:

What does your | father / sister / friend | look like?

What is | he / she | wearing today?

It was a beautiful evening in Malibu. Alex walked with Ana along the beach.

Mona—my wife—is a very selfish person. I'm afraid Brenda is a lot like her.

Scene One

Alex watched Ana's face as they talked. She had a nice smile and an easy laugh. Ana looked very pretty tonight. Alex thought about his wife Mona. The two women were very different.

ALEX How about a walk on the beach? It's still early.

ANA Well, it is a beautiful evening. Okay, let's take a walk.

ALEX I want to thank you, Ana. Willy's happy when he's with you. He doesn't laugh a lot these days.

ANA Yes, he's a sad little boy.

ALEX Willy misses his mother a lot.

ANA What is she like?

ALEX Mona—my wife—is a very selfish person. I'm afraid Brenda is a lot like her.

ANA Brenda is young. I remember when I was sixteen. I wasn't nice then. I thought about boys all the time, especially the Beatles.

ALEX Ha! I guess all fathers worry about their daughters. Here are the steps to your house, Ana.

ANA Thanks, Alex.

ALEX Maybe I can see you tomorrow? Let's go swimming.

ANA Maybe, Alex. Maybe.

Questions

1 Who looks pretty tonight?
2 Is Willy a happy child?
3 Who's selfish?
4 Who did Ana think about when she was young?
5 Is Alex going to see Ana tomorrow?

Tell me, what's so special about her?
We don't know her at all.

Questions

1 Is Mona Stern a beautiful woman?
2 Did Brenda want her father to get married?
3 Is Ana a nice person?
4 What are Alex and Ana doing?
5 Who's going to find out about Ana?

Speechwork

1 It's still early.

2 No, not really.

3 We don't know her at all.

Scene Two

Brenda sat on the deck. She watched her father and Ana as they walked along the beach. Ana was pretty, Brenda thought, but her mother was beautiful. Her father liked Ana, and Willy did too. But Brenda didn't want a new mother.

WILLY   Aren't you going to help me clean the table, Brenda?
BRENDA   Later. I want to finish my ice cream.
WILLY   Didn't you like her, Brenda? Isn't Ana really nice?
BRENDA   Tell me, what's so special about her? We don't know her at all.
WILLY   Well, I don't care. She's my friend.
BRENDA   Yeah, and Dad's friend too. Look at them. They're walking on the beach.
WILLY   Gee, do you think he likes her?
BRENDA   Yeah. I don't like this at all. I'm going to find out about this Ana Cruz.
WILLY   What are you going to do, Brenda? Huh, Brenda?

Signs and Warnings

What do these signs mean?

A

B

C

D

A Match the sign to the warning.

1 You can't open this door.
2 You can't park near the corner.
3 You can't smoke.
4 You have to stop at a red light.
5 You can't drive over 25 miles per hour.
6 You have to use the stairs when there's a fire.

E

F

B What are you going to do?

1 The speed limit is 10 miles an hour. Are you going to drive fast or slowly?
2 The traffic light is yellow. Are you going to stop immediately?
3 There's a fire in the building. Are you going to run quickly to the elevators?
4 The hospital sign says *No Smoking*. Are you going to smoke secretly?

C Where are you going to put these things—below the kitchen sink, in a locked cabinet, or on a high shelf?

Hearabout *Follow the rules*

Brenda found this parking ticket on the car last week.

Listen to the conversation between Brenda and her father. Write or check (✓) the missing information.

VIOLATION   35   336   026   2

Vehicle identified below

N
U
M
B
E
R   ☐ ☐ ☐ ▪ ☐ ☐

| T Y P E | *sta wag* ☐ | *truck* ☐ | *car* ☐ | **Color** |

☐ *am*
☐ *pm*   **Time**   **Date**

Place

In violation of

no parking ☐   *no standing* ☐   *no stopping* ☐

Fine

☐ $10   ☐ $25   ☐ $50   ☐ $75

Speakabout

There's a sign up ahead, but you don't see it. Your friend sees the sign and gives you a warning. Talk about one of the signs on the opposite page.

Cues:	*You*	*Your friend*	*Cues:*
		Point out the sign.	Look at that sign! Don't you see that sign?
What sign? What does it say?	Show surprise.		
		Tell about the sign.	It's a _____ sign. It says _____.
Oh, I guess I can't _____. Really? Then I have to _____.	Follow the rule.		

Ana waited anxiously. Ken Matthews might telephone.

> *Are you disappointed?*
> *Did you expect someone else?*

Scene One

The early morning sunshine woke Ana up. The telephone was next to her. Ken Matthews might call anytime. But the telephone didn't ring.

Ana went into the kitchen and opened the cabinets. On the shelves, there were many boxes and cans of food. In the freezer, Ana found packages of frozen vegetables and meat. A can of coffee was on the counter next to the stove. A few minutes later, Ana heard a knock on the door. It might be Ken.

ALEX   Hello? Hello! Ana, are you up yet?
ANA   Oh . . . hi, Alex.
ALEX   Are you disappointed? Did you expect someone else?
ANA   Oh, no. I'm happy to see you, Alex.
ALEX   Hey, is that *real* coffee on the stove?
ANA   Yes, of course. Would you like a cup?
ALEX   I'd love some coffee, and I'd like to take you for a swim. See, I brought Brenda's suit.
ANA   Okay. But where are the kids?
ALEX   They're sleeping. We can meet them later on the beach.

Questions

1 Did Ana get a telephone call last night?
2 Was there food in the house? Where?
3 Who was at the door?
4 Does Ana drink instant coffee?
5 Where are Brenda and Willy?

> **Look, there are some papers here. And a report on the . . . the LILAC project.**

Scene Two

📼 Brenda didn't sleep late this morning. She got dressed quickly and woke up Willy. Brenda needed Willy's help. Brenda and Willy went out the back door and over the hill to Ana's house. Brenda carefully opened the bedroom window. She pushed Willy into the room.

BRENDA Now, open the door for me, Willy, and let me in.

WILLY Brenda, Ana's my friend. We shouldn't be here.

BRENDA Do what I tell you, Willy. Look around the living room.

WILLY Hey, there's a briefcase here. It's Ana's.

BRENDA Give it to me, Willy. Look, there are some papers here. And a report on the . . . the LILAC project. Look who wrote it. Dr. Karl Jurgens *and* Dr. Ana Cruz.

WILLY So Ana's a scientist.

BRENDA Yeah, but she said she was a secretary. And this is a government report. It's a *secret*, Willy.

WILLY Why does Ana do secret work, Brenda?

BRENDA I don't know. She might be a spy, Willy. C'mon. Let's get out of here.

Questions

1 Did Brenda get up early?
2 Where did Willy and Brenda go?
3 What did they find in the black briefcase?
4 Who wrote the secret report?
5 Is Ana a spy?

Speechwork

1 *Would you* like a cup of coffee? [wʊdžə]
2 *Would you* like to take a swim? [wʊdžə]

Present Modals—MIGHT, SHOULD

Ana has a secret report.	Maybe she's She might be	a spy.
There's a knock on the door. It might be		Ken. Alex.
Should you smoke in a hospital? No, you shouldn't.		

I might he might they should she should	+ Verb

should not → shouldn't

A Tell about choices with *might.*
Give advice with *should.*

1 Willy has a stomachache.

   stay in bed
   take an alka-seltzer

   Willy might stay in bed or he
   might take an alka-seltzer.
   I think he should take an alka-
   seltzer.

2 Ken needs to help Ana.
   telephone her
   go to her house

3 Willy misses his mother.
   write her a letter
   call her

4 Alex's car isn't working well.
   buy a new car
   fix the old car

5 Brenda has a backache.
   lie in the sun
   take two aspirin

● **What *should* or *shouldn't* you do**
when you. . . ?

1 have a headache
2 get a parking ticket
3 break a leg
4 get a present
5 have a test
6 get a party invitation
7 forget an appointment

B Willy is going to celebrate his thirteenth birthday next month. Brenda and
Alex are talking about presents for Willy.

BRENDA It's Willy's birthday next month. What are
   we going to get him?
ALEX   I'm going to buy him a watch. What about
   you?
BRENDA Oh, I don't know. I might give him a book
   or maybe the new Michael Jackson record.

● **A family member or friend is going to have a birthday (anniversary, gradua-**
tion) soon.

What are you going to give [him / her / them] ?

C A friend is asking your advice. What should he/she wear. . . ?

1 to apply for a job in a bank
   You should wear a dark blue
   suit, a white shirt, and a tie.
   You shouldn't wear bluejeans.
2 to go to a football game
3 to meet his girlfriend's parents

4 to go to the theater
5 to go to a rock concert
6 to apply for a job in a school
7 to go to Burger Queen
8 to eat at an expensive restaurant

1 *Give advice*

Alex isn't feeling well. He's at the doctor's office now.

Listen to the conversation. Listen again and write the missing words.

DOCTOR How are you feeling?

ALEX Lousy. I have a _____ pain here, in my stomach.

DOCTOR Hm. Do you have a _____ now?

ALEX Yeah, and it really _____.

DOCTOR Tell me, Alex, _____ you _____ six glasses of _____ every day?

ALEX Well, no, I _____.

DOCTOR You know, you _____ drink a lot of water. And you _____ eat fresh fruit.

ALEX I know you're right. But please, give me some medicine for my stomach.

Role Play: Alex has a toothache. Give advice to Alex.

Start with: Do you have a toothache now?

For good health . . .

Drink six glasses of water every day. Eat fresh fruit.

Brush your teeth after every meal. Don't eat a lot of candy.

2 *Make choices*

Brenda and Maria are discussing future plans.

BRENDA What are you going to do when you finish school?

MARIA I'm not sure. I might go to college or I might join the army.

BRENDA Really? Well, I'm not going to go to school. I'm going to get a job and make money.

● **Tell about *your* future plans, like this:**

I'm going to	go to school. get a job.	I'm sure.
I might study or work. I'm not sure.		

It's getting cloudy on the beach. It might rain soon.

Scene One

 Brenda went into her bedroom and closed the door. She started to read the secret report.

Slowly, Willy walked down the steps to the beach. He sat down on the sand next to Ana.

ANA You're so quiet, Willy. What's the matter?

WILLY Oh, nothing. Where's Dad?

ANA He's swimming. You should go for a swim now, Willy. It's getting cloudy.

WILLY Yeah. It might rain soon. It rained a lot last week too.

ANA I thought it never rained in southern California.

WILLY Sometimes it rains a lot. It's a problem. The hills can't hold the water. We have landslides around here.

ANA C'mon. Let's swim before it rains.

Questions

1 Where did Brenda go? Why?
2 Who did Willy meet on the beach?
3 What is Willy thinking about?
4 Is it a sunny day?
5 What can happen when it rains a lot?

I can't believe it.
Ana, a scientist?

Scene Two

🔊 The rain came down hard. Brenda heard the front door open and close. Alex and Willy were back from the beach. Brenda picked up the LILAC report and went into the living room.

BRENDA Dad, look at this.

ALEX What's that, Brenda?

WILLY It's a government report. See, Dad? Ana wrote it.

ALEX Who's Dr. Jurgens? What's this LILAC project? I can't believe it. Ana, a scientist?

BRENDA It's true, Dad. Ana and Dr. Jurgens worked on a secret formula. It's a dangerous chemical.

ALEX Where did you get this report?

BRENDA From Ana's house. Is Ana a spy? She lied to us. She's not a secretary, Dad.

ALEX I don't know the answer, Brenda, but I can find out.

WILLY Where are you going, Dad?

ALEX To Los Angeles. I want to find out more about this LILAC project.

Questions

1 Who came into the house?
2 Where did Brenda go?
3 What did she show her father?
4 Did Ana lie to the Sterns?
5 Who's going to Los Angeles? Why?

Speechwork

1 Where are you going? [wɛryə]
2 What are you doing? [wətšə]
3 When are you leaving? [wɛnyə]

At the supermarket

What would you like to buy today?

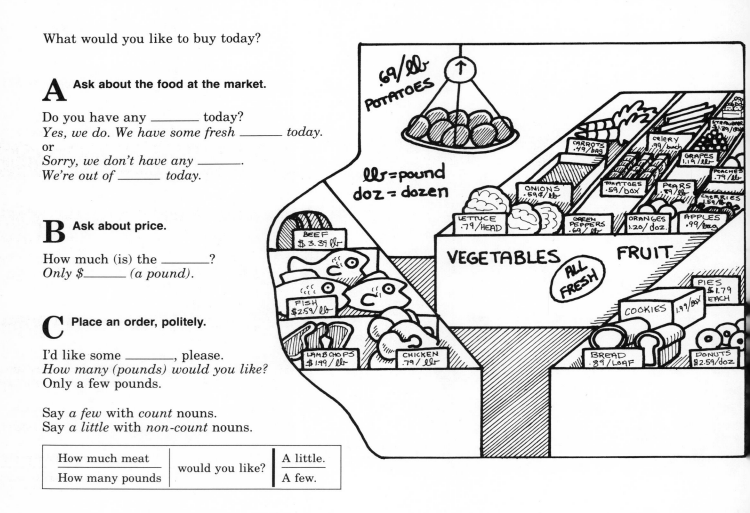

A Ask about the food at the market.

Do you have any _____ today?
Yes, we do. We have some fresh _____ today.
or
Sorry, we don't have any _____.
We're out of _____ today.

B Ask about price.

How much (is) the _____?
Only $_____ (a pound).

C Place an order, politely.

I'd like some _____, please.
How many (pounds) would you like?
Only a few pounds.

Say *a few* with *count* nouns.
Say *a little* with *non-count* nouns.

How much meat	would you like?	A little.
How many pounds		A few.

D What's the "best buy" for your money? Which *should* you get?

16 ounces = 1 pound
1 kilo = 2.2 pounds

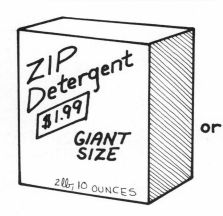

or

THE WEATHER REPORT

What's the climate like in southern California?

Southern California is one of the few places in the world where you can ski in the morning and surf in the afternoon. As you travel the short distance from the high mountains to the low deserts to the beaches, the temperature can change 30 to 40 degrees. Winters are mild, with rain sometimes from January through March. Summers are hot and dry.

What's the weather like today?

The sun is shining in Los Angeles, with a high temperature of 82 degrees. It isn't warm in San Francisco. There are some clouds overhead. The temperature is 62 degrees.

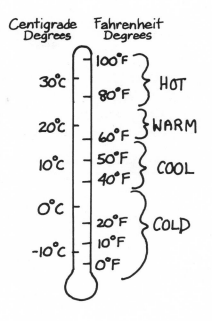

In the U.S.

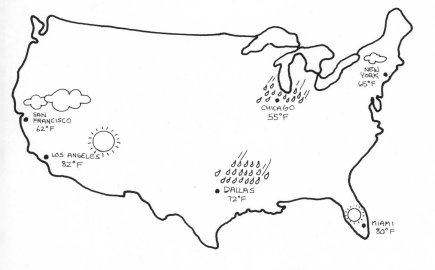

. . . and around the world.

City	Temperature	Weather
Cairo	97°F	sunny
Moscow	30°F	snow
São Paulo	72°F	rain
Tokyo	58°F	cloudy

Thinkabout

	True	False		True	False
1 January is hot and dry in southern California.		✓	3 The sun isn't shining in São Paulo.		
2 It might rain in New York and Tokyo.			4 It isn't raining hard in Cairo now.		

Talkabout

1 What's the weather like in your country right now?

2 Does it usually (rain in April)?

3 When is it hot? cold? cool? warm? dry? wet?

4 What's your favorite season—fall, winter, spring or summer?

5 What time of year do people play sports? stay indoors?

Largo is leaving the Surfer Motel, but he'll be back. He won't be away long.

This needle will help you sleep.

Scene One

🔊 It was evening and Largo was hungry. He tied a handkerchief around Ken's mouth. Ken was quiet now. Largo left the motel. Ken was hungry and thirsty too. Largo didn't give him any food or water all day.

When Largo returned, he took the handkerchief from Ken's mouth.

KEN   Have a nice dinner, Largo?

LARGO Just a steak and a large bottle of California wine. You're hungry, aren't you, Matthews?

KEN   Oh, I had a big breakfast two days ago. Don't worry about me.

LARGO That's not funny, Matthews. You are beginning to bore me. But I do have something for you.

KEN   For me? Hey, what's that? A needle?

LARGO Yes, my friend. This needle will help you sleep. But I'll be back for you. First, I need to make a visit to Dr. Cruz.

Questions

1 What did Largo do with the handkerchief?
2 Why did Largo leave?
3 Did Largo give Ken any breakfast?
4 Is Ken going to go to sleep? Why?
5 Where is Largo going?

There might be a flood. Maybe a landslide.

ROAD CLOSED

Scene Two

🎮 The rain was heavy and the road was like a river. Largo saw a sign—Malibu, five miles. Two police cars were up ahead. Largo stopped his car.

LARGO   What's the problem, officer?
OFFICER The rain is pretty heavy, sir. There might be a flood. Maybe a landslide.
LARGO   Well, I have to go to . . . uh . . . my house. It's up the road a few miles.
OFFICER It's dangerous with all this rain.
LARGO   I have to go there. My . . . uh . . . sister Ana is all alone.
OFFICER Well, the road will be okay for about an hour or so. Get your sister out of the house. These landslides are dangerous.
LARGO   Don't worry. I'll be careful.

Questions

1 What was the road like?
2 What did the sign say?
3 Who did Largo talk to?
4 Is the road safe?
5 Who's in the house up the road?

Speechwork

1 *I'll* be careful. [ayl]
2 *He'll* be back. [hiyl]
3 *It'll* help you sleep. [ɪɒəl]

WILL, WON'T Future

Where	will you meet me? I'll	be in front of the cinema.
When		meet you at seven.

Largo left the motel.	He's going to get some food.
	He'll be back in an hour.
	He won't be back until ten.

I will	
he will	+ Verb
they will	

will	→	**'ll**
will not		**won't**

A Brenda and Maria are making plans to meet.

BRENDA   Let's go to a movie.
MARIA   What time?
BRENDA   I'll meet you at seven.
MARIA   Where will you meet me?
BRENDA   I'll be in front of the Center Cinema.

● **Make plans with your classmate. Choose a time and a place in *this* city.**

1 restaurant
2 department store
3 disco
4 football game
5 concert

B Elvira is talking to her supervisor at the Berkeley Science Laboratory.

SUPERVISOR   Where are you going, Elvira?
ELVIRA   To the bathroom. I'll be back in five minutes. I won't be away long.

● **Ask and answer, like this:**

Where are you going?
When will you be back?

I'm going to	get some coffee. buy cigarettes. shop for shoes. see friends. visit my family.	I'll be back in	twenty minutes. a half hour. three hours. four days. two weeks.
I won't be back until	one o'clock. two-fifteen. four o'clock. Sunday. March 10th.		

C Maria is asking Brenda about her travel plans.

very sure	I'm going to . . .
sure	I'll . . .
not sure	I might . . .
very sure	I won't . . .

MARIA   Are you going to take a vacation this year?
BRENDA   Yes, I'm going to travel to Europe with my mother.
MARIA   What places will you visit?
BRENDA   I think we'll go to England and Ireland.
MARIA   When will you go?
BRENDA   Well, we might go in July, or maybe August.
MARIA   How long will you stay?
BRENDA   For about a month. We won't stay after August. I have school in September.

● **Interview a classmate. Ask about his or her travel plans.**

1 *Disagree strongly*

There's a sign on the door of room number 23. It says *Do Not Disturb.* The maids at the Surfer Motel want to clean the room.

Listen to the conversation. Listen again and write the missing words.

FIRST MAID   We can't go in there. Don't you see the sign?

SECOND MAID But we _____ clean the room now. We _____ _____ clean it every morning.

FIRST MAID   Well, we can't now. The _____ says *Do Not Disturb.*

SECOND MAID Let's come _____ this afternoon. _____ clean it then.

FIRST MAID   You can, but not me. I _____ work late. I have to get home _____.

SECOND MAID Room 24 is empty. Let's clean that one now.

Role Play: You and your friend are at the bank, post office, or supermarket. There's a long line of people in front of you. Your friend wants to wait, but you don't.

Start with: We can't wait. Don't you see all those people?

End with: I won't wait. I have to get back to work/school.

2 *Remind someone to do something*

Maria found this note from her mother. Then she left the house and went to work. Later Maria's mother calls her at Burger Queen.

MOTHER Don't forget to buy some onions.

MARIA   No, I won't forget. I'll get three pounds of onions.

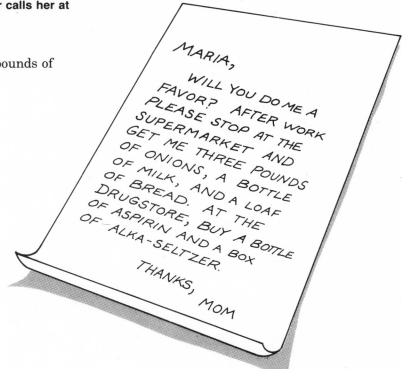

MARIA,

WILL YOU DO ME A FAVOR? AFTER WORK PLEASE STOP AT THE SUPERMARKET AND GET ME THREE POUNDS OF ONIONS, A BOTTLE OF MILK, AND A LOAF OF BREAD. AT THE DRUGSTORE, BUY A BOTTLE OF ASPIRIN AND A BOX OF ALKA-SELTZER.

THANKS, MOM

• Ask about the other items in the note.

Alex is at the Los Angeles Public Library. He'll try to find out about the LILAC project.

Scene One

🔊 It was almost four-thirty when Alex reached the library. He put an old newspaper over his head and ran through the rain to the front door. Alex looked for the reference desk.

ALEX   Excuse me. Do you have a copy of *Who's Who*?

LIBRARIAN   Here it is. What name do you want to look up?

ALEX   Ana Cruz. Dr. Ana Cruz. She's from San Francisco.

LIBRARIAN   No, I don't find her name.

ALEX   What about Jurgens? Is Dr. Karl Jurgens in *Who's Who*?

LIBRARIAN   Here it is. Yes, he's a famous scientist at the Berkeley Laboratory. He works for the government on chemical weapons. Hmmm . . . Dr. Karl Jurgens . . .

ALEX   Do you know about him?

LIBRARIAN   I remember now. Yes, he was in an accident. I read about it in the San Francisco newspaper.

ALEX   Do you have that newspaper?

LIBRARIAN   It's in the back room. I'll get it.

Questions

1 When did Alex arrive at the library?
2 What was the weather like?
3 Is Ana Cruz's name in *Who's Who*?
4 What does Alex find out about Dr. Jurgens?
5 What's in the back room?

Scene Two

Alex looked out the window. The rain was really coming down. Alex looked at his watch. It was almost five o'clock. The library will close soon, he thought.

LIBRARIAN Here, I've got the newspaper. Look on page 17.

ALEX You're right. There was a car accident, and Jurgens was killed.

LIBRARIAN Read the last part. It says something about Dr. Ana Cruz.

ALEX Yes, the guard at the Berkeley Lab said she left with Jurgens that night. The police can't find her. They want to ask her some questions.

LIBRARIAN I'm sorry. It's five o'clock. I'll have to close the library now. Where are you from?

ALEX Oh, the Malibu area.

LIBRARIAN The Malibu area! Didn't you listen to the radio? There are flood warnings in Malibu. Maybe a landslide.

ALEX My kids! I left my kids alone. I've got to get home right away!

Questions

1 What was the story on page 17 about?
2 Who are the police looking for?
3 What time does the library close?
4 What warning was on the radio?
5 What is Alex worried about?

Speechwork

1 I've got to get home right away. [gaɒə]
2 I've got to close the library. [gaɒə]

Opening and closing hours

A Will the bank be open now? Ask about times, like this:

When is the bank open?

It's open from nine in the morning to three in the afternoon, Monday through Friday.

What about Saturday and Sunday?
It's closed on weekends.

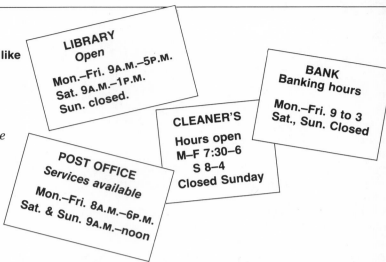

LIBRARY
Open
Mon.–Fri. 9A.M.–5P.M.
Sat. 9A.M.–1P.M.
Sun. closed.

BANK
Banking hours
Mon.–Fri. 9 to 3
Sat., Sun. Closed

CLEANER'S
Hours open
M–F 7:30–6
S 8–4
Closed Sunday

POST OFFICE
Services available
Mon.–Fri. 8A.M.–6P.M.
Sat. & Sun. 9A.M.–noon

B Tell what you *have got to* do.

| I | have to
have ('ve) got to | get to the bank. |
|---|---|---|

It's Thursday at 4:45. You've got to deposit some money.
I've got to get to the bank. It'll close in fifteen minutes.

Time right now:		Things to do:
Thursday	4:45 P.M.	deposit money
Saturday	12:30 P.M.	return a book
Tuesday	7:45 A.M.	mail a package
Monday	5:40 P.M.	pick up a suit
Wednesday	8:55 A.M.	cash a check
Sunday	11:50 A.M.	buy stamps

C Tell what you can or can't do on a holiday.

You have to . . .

1 return a book
2 get a money order
3 buy a loaf of bread
4 buy a roll of film
5 get a passport

The library won't be open.

Hearabout Leave a message

Maria Gomez received a telephone call at work. Her supervisor took this message.

Listen to the conversation. Write the missing parts.

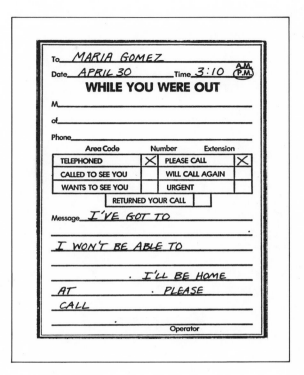

> To __MARIA GOMEZ__
> Date __APRIL 30__ Time __3:10__ (A.M. / **P.M.**)
> ## WHILE YOU WERE OUT
> M_____
> of_____
> Phone_____
>
> | | Area Code | Number | Extension |
> |---|---|---|---|
> | TELEPHONED | ☒ | PLEASE CALL | ☒ |
> | CALLED TO SEE YOU | | WILL CALL AGAIN | |
> | WANTS TO SEE YOU | | URGENT | |
> | | RETURNED YOUR CALL | | |
>
> Message __I'VE GOT TO__
> _____.
> __I WON'T BE ABLE TO__
> _____
> _____. __I'LL BE HOME__
> __AT__ _____. __PLEASE__
> __CALL__
> _____._____
> Operator

Speakabout

Leave a message for a friend. Explain you have to do something and won't be able to meet him or her.

Cues:	You	The other person	Cues:
I'd like to leave a message for _____. My name is _____.	Ask to leave a message. Give your name.		
		Ask about the message.	What's the message, please? What do you want me to tell _____?
I've got to _____. I'll call (name) _____. Please call me _____.	Give the message.		
		Ask for telephone number.	Can you give me your telephone number? What's your telephone number, please?
It's _____. My number is _____. And thanks./Thank you.	Give information. Say thanks.		

The maids should clean room 23. The manager is going to open the door.

> *Get me a knife. We have to cut these ropes.*

Scene One

 It was late in the afternoon. The *Do Not Disturb* sign was still on the door of room number 23. One of the maids returned with the motel manager. He knocked several times, then opened the door.

MAID   Look at that man! He's tied to the chair.

MANAGER Get me a knife. We have to cut these ropes. Take the handkerchief out of his mouth.

KEN   Oh, oh, where am I?

MANAGER You're at the Surfer Motel. Where's that other man?

KEN   Largo! I have to find Largo!

MAID   Hey, what's this card on the table? Are you a U.S. agent, Mr. Matthews?

MANAGER I'll call the police, Mr. Matthews.

KEN   No, I'm all right. Give me the telephone.

Questions

1 Why did the maids return to the room?
2 Where was Ken?
3 Who needed a knife? Why?
4 Where's Ken's ID card?
5 Who's going to make a phone call?

34

*Where's Largo now?
Is he coming here?
What will I do?*

Scene Two

📼 Ken's head ached. He felt a sharp pain in his right arm.
The pain was from the needle.

Ken took the telephone from the motel manager. He dialed
Ana's number. The phone rang several times before Ana an-
swered.

KEN Ana, it's Ken. Ken Matthews.

ANA Where are you? Why didn't you come last night?

KEN Largo found me. Then he tied me up. But I'm okay.

ANA Ken, where's Largo now? Is he coming here? What will
I do?

KEN I'll be there soon, Ana. Can you get away from the
house?

ANA Where can I go? It's raining hard, and I don't have a
car.

KEN Think, Ana. What's around there?

ANA Well, there's a family next door. No, I can't go there.
Then they'll be in danger too.

KEN All right. Lock the door. I won't be long.

ANA Ken, hurry. Please hurry.

Questions

1 Did Ken's arm hurt? Why?
2 Who did Ken call?
3 Where is Largo now?
4 Should Ana leave the Malibu house?
5 Who lives in the house next door?

Speechwork

1 *Give me* the telephone. [gɪmiy]
2 Why *didn't you* come last night? [dɪnčə]

Integration

Are you going to visit Europe?	We	'll visit England.
		might visit Ireland.

He's late for work. He might take a taxi or a bus.

I need a secretary.	You	should	hire a	good typist.
		shouldn't		careless person.

 Brenda is talking to her mother about their trip to Europe. Mona is looking at this travel plan. Complete the telephone conversation.

KALT TRAVEL AGENCY
New York, New York 10021

* *

Aug 1	Depart NY
Aug 2-9	London Hilton
Aug 9-12	Drive to Bath & visit Roman ruins
Aug 12-15	Drive to Exeter & Amesbury—visit Stonehenge
Aug 15-25	???
Aug 25	Return to NY

BRENDA   When are we going to leave for London?
MONA   On August _____.
BRENDA   How long _____?
MONA   About a week. Then we'll rent a car and travel around England.
BRENDA   What places _____?
MONA   First we'll go to Bath and then to Exeter and Amesbury.
BRENDA   Are _____ Ireland?
MONA   We might. We can decide on the 15th.
BRENDA   When _____ to New York?
MONA   On August 25th. You won't be late for school.

B **What should or shouldn't you do in these situations?**

1 You get up late for work. This is the third time you will be late this month. Should you . . . ?

a take a taxi and pay $10
b take a bus and apologize to your supervisor
c stay home and call in sick

2 Your friend cooks dinner for you. You think the food is terrible. Should you . . . ?

a be honest and say it's awful
b eat it all and say it's wonderful
c eat some of the dinner and say you are feeling sick today

C **Tell about you. Check (√) Yes or No.**

Are you a . . . ?

	Yes	No
fast thinker		
slow learner		
careful writer		
hard worker		
patient listener		
polite speaker		
neat dresser		
good cook		

● **Ask your classmate, like this:**
Are you a fast thinker?
Do you think fast?

● **You own a business and you need to hire an assistant. What kind of person should you hire?**

1 a polite speaker
2 a quick learner
3 a good typist

What about . . . ?

1 a driver for your company car
2 a sales representative
3 a receptionist

1 *Refuse permission*

Ken Matthews drove slowly. The road was filled with water because of the heavy rain. Up ahead he saw police cars.
Listen to the conversation. Listen again and write the missing words.

POLICE Hey, mister. You can't go up that road. It's almost flooded.

KEN I'm a U.S. agent. I _____ _____ get to Ocean Beach Drive.

POLICE You _____ go. It's dangerous, sir. There _____ _____ a landslide.

KEN Did you see a _____ man with a mustache? He's driving a _____ _____ Buick.

POLICE Yeah, he wanted _____ _____ his sister. He said her name was Ana.

KEN I _____ _____ to find that man. I'm _____ _____ 214 Ocean Beach Drive.

POLICE The rescue helicopter _____ _____ here soon. We can take you to the house.

KEN No, I can't wait. When the helicopter arrives, come and get us.

Role Play: You are a police officer. Give or refuse permission to enter the Malibu area to. . . .

a an eighty-year-old woman. She wants to get her cat.
b a young man. He wants to get his wife and baby.

Start with: You can't go up that road. It's almost flooded.

2 *Describe a lost object*

Willy and Brenda are upstairs. Willy is upset. Brenda tries to help him.

BRENDA What's the matter?
WILLY I can't find my history notebook.
BRENDA Did you look in your bookbag? It might be there.

● **Make short conversations about Willy's other things.**

Willy can't find his . . .	It might be . . .	
leather wallet wool sweater	in	the closet the drawer
tennis shoe cotton sock	on	the desk the chair
raincoat sunglasses	under	the bed the couch

Scene One

Brenda looked out the window. It was very dark. The rain was coming down hard. Brenda was worried. Her father wasn't home yet.

Willy turned on the radio.

BRENDA   Turn it louder, Willy. I want to hear the weather report.

WILLY   Is Dad okay, Brenda? It's really late, and he's not home.

BRENDA   Shhh! Be quiet, or I won't be able to hear the announcer.

ANNOUNCER Weather Bulletin. Heavy storms hit the southern California area again today. All roads are closed because of flooding. There is danger of landslides. Repeat. There is danger of flooding and landslides . . .

BRENDA   Shut it off, Willy. I'm afraid. Dad, where are you? Please come home safely.

Brenda and Willy are listening to the weather report. They are worried about their father.

Be quiet, or I won't be able to hear the announcer.

Questions

1 Was Alex in the house?
2 What's on the radio?
3 Why aren't the roads open?
4 What's the danger?
5 Who's afraid? Why?

Scene Two

📼 Willy was afraid too. He went into his bedroom. The seashell from Ana was on the desk. Willy remembered what Ana told him. Put the shell to your ear and all your troubles will go away.

Willy put the shell next to his ear. He didn't hear the ocean.

BRENDA   What are you doing, Willy?

WILLY   Brenda, I can't hear anything. I can't hear the ocean. This is a special shell. Ana said so.

BRENDA   Give it to me, Willy. You're right. I can't hear anything.

WILLY   But I did before. I heard the ocean.

BRENDA   What's this? There's some paper in the shell. Hey, there's some writing on it. Look at this chemical formula.

WILLY   Is it a secret formula, like the LILAC project?

BRENDA   How do I know? I don't study chemistry in school.

WILLY   Show it to Dad, Brenda. He'll know.

BRENDA   Yeah, Dad should know. But where is Dad?

Questions

1 What was on Willy's desk?
2 Did Willy hear the ocean?
3 Why is the shell special?
4 What's on the paper?
5 Who should know about the formula?

Speechwork

1 All roads are closed *because of* flooding. [biykəzv]
2 There's *danger of* landslides. [deyndžəv]

Brenda, I can't hear anything. I can't hear the ocean.

Eating out

What would you like to order?

A Place your order, like this:

I'd like	— to have to order	the soup.

The Garden Restaurant
MENU

Appetizers

onion soup	1.75
vegetable soup	1.75
melon	2.00
tomato juice	1.50

Main Courses

Roast chicken	5.95	Fried chicken	6.95
Sirloin steak	12.95	Bluefish	7.95
Lamb chops	7.95	Lobster	15.00
Roast beef	9.95		

With choice of two vegetables

Boiled potato   carrots, peas, corn
French fries   spinach, green beans

Salads

Mixed green	1.25
Fruit salad	1.50
Spinach salad	1.75

Desserts

Chocolate cake	1.75
Apple pie	1.75
Ice cream	1.50

Beverages

Coffee	1.00	Beer	2.00
Tea	1.00	Glass of wine	1.50
Soda	1.25		

WAITER May I take your order?
YOU First, I'd like the onion soup. Then I'd like to have the sirloin steak.
WAITER What vegetables would you like?
YOU French fries and peas. Oh, and a mixed green salad.

WAITER Would you like your salad before or after your meal?
YOU Before, please. And I'll order dessert later.
WAITER Anything else?
YOU Yes, I'd like a beer, please.

B Take an order from your classmate. Complete the waiter's check with prices. Then compute the tax and total the bill.

CHECK   Table _____
Date _____
Waiter _____
**************************** price

plus 5% tax _____
TOTAL _____

The Classified Section

- Do you need a job?

- Are you going to buy or sell something?

- What did you lose or find?

- Do you like to go to auctions?

Los Angeles Times

Classified Section

March 12, 1987

Situations wanted

Italian girl, 18, newly arrived U.S., needs employment with friendly family in exchange for room and meals. Will take care of young children. Good cook. Call 217-4109. Ask for Pia.

College student, male, is looking for part-time work, 10–15 hours per week. Careful worker with office experience. Can type 55 wpm. Telephone 423-8314. George.

Well-educated young woman wants full-time work in bank or doctor's office. Excellent skills. Can speak Spanish and French well. Fluent in English. Write: M. Flores, P.O. Box 218, San Francisco, CA 94413.

Want to Buy

We pay high prices for new and used bedroom and living room furniture. CALL "AS TIME GOES BY" 714-8199.

USED APPLIANCES
Sell us your old refrigerators, stoves, and washing machines. We pay cash and pick up. Telephone THE KITCHEN STORE 927-5530

Want to Sell

FOR SALE—used furniture and kitchen appliances—famous brand names at cheap prices. The Home Store - 86 Main St. Santa Monica. OPEN 10–8 daily.

Articles for Trade

Lost and Found

Brown briefcase—left on Number 4 bus last Monday night. Will give $100 reward to finder. CALL 615-2157, after 6 p.m.

FOUND—new gold watch. Can you identify the initials on back of the watch? Telephone Carol 350-2613.

Auctions

Persian and Chinese Rugs in a variety of sizes and colors—CASH ONLY. Sunday 2–6. The Garden Motel, Santa Monica Boulevard.

FAMOUS ART COLLECTION 17th and 18th Century PAINTINGS

Thinkabout

Match:

1 You want to employ a person who speaks French or Spanish well.

2 Your stove is old and you need money to buy a new one.

3 You lost your watch on the bus.

4 You need a person to take care of your children.

a Call The Kitchen Store.

b Telephone Pia at 217-4109.

c Write M. Flores in San Francisco.

d Contact Carol at 350-2613.

- **Write a notice for something you lost or found or you want to buy or sell.**

```
        NOTICE



```

FOR SALE — 1983
Red Honda in excellent condition. Radio works well and the tires are brand new. Make an offer. Greg. Telephone 486-3216 evenings.

NOTICE
I lost a large green bookbag in the cafeteria last Tuesday. There's a new math book and a gold pen inside. $10 reward. CALL Brad 714-3002.

Now open that briefcase and take out all the papers.

Largo saw two houses. The smaller one was Ana's house.

Scene One

🔊 Slowly, Largo drove his car along Ocean Beach Drive. The wind was stronger now, and the sky was darker. There were lights in the house up ahead. The number of the house was 212 Ocean Beach Drive. Number 214 was next door. It was the smaller house.

Largo got out of the car and found the wooden steps to Ana's house. The steps were loose because of the heavy rain. The hill was a sea of mud.

Largo looked in the window and saw Ana. She was alone.

ANA   Who's there? Ken, is that you?
LARGO Thank you for opening the door, Dr. Cruz.
ANA   I don't know you. Who are you?
LARGO This gun should help you remember. You know who I am, Dr. Cruz, don't you?
ANA   Largo? You're Largo, aren't you?
LARGO Yes, and we have some business to discuss. The LILAC formula. Remember?

Questions

1 Did Largo drive slowly? Why?
2 Who lives in the small house?
3 Were the steps loose? Why?
4 Was Ken at the door? Who was?
5 What does Largo want?

Scene Two

🔊 Ana's living room was a mess. Largo opened all the drawers of the desk. He turned them over on the floor, but he didn't find the LILAC formula.

LARGO What's in that briefcase?

ANA Nothing. I don't know what you want.

LARGO Oh, yes you do. I want that formula. Now open that briefcase and take out all the papers.

ANA See, there's no formula in this briefcase. I don't have the formula.

LARGO I know you have it. The experiment was a success. Jurgens told me.

ANA I don't know anything about it.

LARGO Don't lie to me, Dr. Cruz. And I can help you remember.

Questions

1 Was the living room a mess? Why?
2 Who turned over the drawers?
3 Was the LILAC formula in the briefcase?
4 Did Ana have the formula?
5 Where is it?

Speechwork

1 The smaller one was Ana's house.

2 The wind was stronger.

3 The sky was darker.

Adjectives—Comparatives

Is Alex	older younger	than Ana?	Yes, No,	he's 42 and she's 35.

Will it be cooler soon?	Yes, March No, June	is a	colder warmer	month.

An adventure movie is more enjoyable than a violent movie.

short sad	+ er →	shorter sadder
but		
good bad expensive	→	better worse more expensive

A Tell about the story. Make comparatives. Add *-er* to one or two syllable adjectives:

old	older
young →	younger
pretty	prettier

1 Alex is 42 years old.
Ana is 35.
Who's older?

Alex is older than Ana.

2 Largo is 6 feet tall.
Ken is over 6 feet.
Who's taller?

3 Ana is pretty.
Mona is very pretty.
Who's prettier?

4 Willy is 12 years old.
Brenda is 16.
Who's younger?

5 Alex is friendly.
Willy is very friendly.
Who's friendlier?

6 Brenda is smart.
Maria is very smart.
Who's smarter?

B Elvira is listening to the five-day weather forecast on the radio.

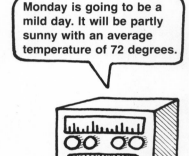

Monday is going to be a mild day. It will be partly sunny with an average temperature of 72 degrees.

Five Day Weather Forecast

Monday	partly sunny	a mild day	72°
Tuesday	sunny	a fine day	75°
Wednesday	cloudy	a dry and cool day	68°
Thursday	rainy	a wet and windy day	70°
Friday	sunny	a perfect day	78°

● **Ask about the weather:**

1 Will it be warmer or cooler on Tuesday? Wednesday? Thursday? Friday?

It will be warmer on Tuesday. The temperature will be 75 degrees.

2 When will the weather be better or worse. . . ?
a on Tuesday or Wednesday
b on Thursday or Friday

● **Tell about the weather in your country.**

1 Which are the colder (hotter, cooler, warmer) months?
2 Which are the wetter (drier) months?

C Give your opinion. Use *more* with adjectives of three or more syllables.

1 Which book is more interesting, a mystery novel or a love story?

2 car/expensive—a Mercedes or a Ford?

3 sport/exciting—football or tennis?

4 vacation/enjoyable—at the beach or in a city?

5 occupation/important—farming or medicine?

6 pet/popular—a dog or a cat?

1 *Make comparisons*

Elvira lives in a city apartment but Bill lives in the suburbs outside of San Francisco. Bill thinks Elvira should move to the country.
Listen to the conversation. Listen again and write the missing words.

BILL   Why do you live in the city? You should move to the country.

ELVIRA I like the city. Life in the city is _____ _____. You can go to movies and theaters, and the shopping is _____.

BILL   Yeah, but it's _____ in the country. There are trees and flowers and the air is _____.

ELVIRA That's true, but it isn't _____ _____ in the country. You know I don't like hiking or fishing.

BILL   Well, it is _____ to live in the country, and it is a lot _____.

ELVIRA No, I won't move. My apartment might be _____ _____, but I'm _____ in the city.

BILL   Don't forget. You can visit me when you want some peace and quiet.

Role Play: Talk about places to live. You choose a place in this city. Your classmate chooses a place *outside* this city.

Start with: You should move to _____.

2 *Tell about differences*

Maria is showing Brenda a photograph of her new boyfriend Mike. Maria's old boyfriend was shy and serious. Mike is different.

BRENDA Mike looks like a nice guy.

MARIA   Yeah, he's a lot nicer than my old boyfriend. Mike is friendlier and funnier. He has a great sense of humor.

● **Ask about friends from home, like this:**
What's your friend like?
Well, he/she is _____ *than I am.*

Is your friend. . . ?

tall/short	outgoing/quiet
young/old	serious/funny
heavy/thin	

Brenda showed her father the paper with the chemical formula.

Willy, Brenda. You two wait here. Stay in the house.

Scene One

 Alex drove the station wagon behind the house. He ran through the thick mud to the back door.

WILLY Dad! Dad, you're back. Look what we found. It was in the shell. Ana gave me this shell, Dad.

ALEX What are you talking about, Willy?

WILLY Show the paper to Dad, Brenda.

ALEX What's this? Hmm. It's some kind of chemical formula.

BRENDA It has to be the LILAC formula. I read about it. The formula is a chemical weapon.

WILLY Dad, Ana's not a spy. Is she, Dad?

ALEX I don't know, Willy. Ana lied to us. She is a scientist and she worked with Dr. Jurgens. The police are looking for her now.

BRENDA What are we going to do, Dad?

ALEX Well, we have to get out of this house. It's all mud outside. There's going to be a landslide.

WILLY But, Dad, what about Ana? We can't leave her here!

Questions

1 Where did Alex park the car?
2 Who gave Willy the shell?
3 What's on the paper?
4 Are the police looking for Ana? Why?
5 Is Willy worried about Ana? Why?

Scene Two

Alex put on his boots and raincoat. The storm was worse. It was raining harder now. The water carried the mud down the hill. Mud was all around the house.

Alex saw a light in Ana's window. Alex had to warn Ana about the landslide.

BRENDA Daddy, we're ready. We have our raincoats and boots.
ALEX Willy, Brenda. You two wait here. Stay in the house.
WILLY Dad, where are you going?
ALEX To Ana's house. Brenda, put the piece of paper back into the shell.
BRENDA Here's the shell, Dad. Can't I go with you?
ALEX No, stay here with your brother. It's safer here.
WILLY Dad, Ana's my friend. She's not a spy, is she, Dad?
ALEX We don't know, son. But Ana's in trouble. Maybe we can help her. Now don't leave the house. I'll be back in a few minutes.

Questions

1 Was the weather worse? Why?
2 Who's going to warn Ana?
3 What did Brenda give to her father?
4 Who has to stay in the house? Why?
5 Will Alex be away long?

Speechwork

1 It's some *kind of* chemical formula. [kayndə]
2 She's some *kind of* spy. [kayndə]

Used Cars

A Which car do you prefer—the more expensive or cheaper one? Ask about the used cars, like this:

Which car. . . ?

1 has the higher (lower) mileage
2 is easier (harder) to drive
3 has the more powerful engine
4 is a lighter (darker) color

5 is more economical (expensive) to drive
6 has the more interesting features
7 is the better value for the price

	1976 Volkswagen	1982 Mustang
mileage	63,642 miles	37,430 miles
transmission	manual shift	automatic shift
power	four cylinders	six cylinders
color	light blue	dark blue
economy	24 miles to the gallon	19 miles to the gallon
features	sunroof radio	convertible radio and tape deck
price	$1250	$2800

B Complete this survey about the transportation in this city.

Check (✓)		Always	Usually	Sometimes	Never
Are the buses	clean?				
	crowded?				
Are the taxis	expensive?				
	safe?				
Are the trains	fast?				
	noisy?				

Who's more polite,	☐ a bus driver	or	☐ a taxi driver?
What's more reliable,	☐ a train	or	☐ a bus?
What's more comfortable,	☐ a train	or	☐ a taxi?
What's more private,	☐ a bus	or	☐ a train?

● Interview a classmate to find out about his or her opinion.

Hearabout   *Rent a car*

Pedro is telephoning the E-Z Rent-A-Car Company.
He wants to reserve a car.

**Listen to the conversation. Write or check (✓) the missing
parts on the registration form.**

**E-Z Rent-A-CAR
Reservation Form**

Name _____

Address _____ Tele _____

Credit Card: ☐ VISA ☐ Am Exp   No. _____

Car: ☐ Ford ☐ Buick ☐ manual ☐ automatic

Model: ☐ sedan ☐ sunroof ☐ convertible   Insurance: $_____

Date of   Time of   ☐ AM Date of
pick up: _____ pick up: _____ ☐ PM return: _____

Rate: ☐ weekend ☐ weekly ☐ daily   TOTAL COST: $_____

Speakabout

**Tell your friend about your new car. Your friend is surprised about
your choice. He likes another model. Explain why your car is better than your friend's choice.**

Cues:	*You*	*Your friend*	*Cues:*
I bought a _____ yesterday. Look at my new _____.	Identify the car.		
		Show surprise. Give your choice.	Why didn't you buy a _____? I think a _____ is a better car.
My car is better because it's faster/ more economical/ cheaper. My car has more interesting features. It has _____.	Give reasons for your choice.		
		Disagree.	I don't think so. A _____ is better because _____.

LANDSLIDE

Alex walked through the heavy rain to Ana's house. The wind was blowing in his face.

> We can look in Ana's window.

Scene One

🔊 Alex took the shell and stepped out into the storm. He looked over the deck. The ocean below was dark and angry. Alex turned on his flashlight. Carefully, he walked through the mud to Ana's house.

From the window, Brenda was watching her father. Quickly, she put on her boots and raincoat.

BRENDA Hurry up, Willy. Put on your raincoat and boots.
WILLY Why? Where are we going?
BRENDA After Dad. We can watch them. We can look in Ana's window.
WILLY Brenda, we shouldn't do that. Dad will be angry. He told us to stay here. You heard him too.
BRENDA Well, you can stay, but I'm going.
WILLY I don't want to stay alone, Brenda. I'm afraid.
BRENDA Well, hurry up then, or I won't wait for you.

Questions

1 Who had the shell?
2 Where did Alex go?
3 Who did Brenda want to watch?
4 What did Alex tell Brenda and Willy to do?
5 Is Brenda going to wait for Willy?

Take the shell and go.
Leave me alone.

Scene Two

Largo was in the bedroom. He was looking for the formula. Ana was too tired and frightened to think. They heard a knock on the door.

Largo hid in the kitchen. He told Ana to answer the door. Largo had a gun, and he was pointing the gun at Ana.

ANA Alex, what are you doing here?

ALEX I have to talk to you. And get you out of here. There's going to be a landslide. It's a river of mud out there.

ANA Alex, go away. I don't want you here.

ALEX Ana, you're in trouble. What's in this seashell? It looks like a chemical formula. What's this all about, Ana?

ANA Please, Alex. Take the shell and go. Leave me alone.

ALEX Did you hear a noise? I heard something. The noise came from the kitchen.

ANA I didn't hear anything. The wind was blowing, that's all. Alex, please. Go now, before it's too late.

Questions

1 Where was Largo? Why?
2 What did Ana and Largo hear?
3 Where did Largo hide?
4 Who made the noise?
5 Did Ana want Alex to stay?

Speechwork

1 The wind *was blowing* in his face. [w(ə)z blowɪn]
2 He *was looking* for the formula. [w(ə)z lʊkɪn]
3 He *was pointing* the gun at Ana. [w(ə)z pɔyntɪn]

51

Past Continuous

Alex was	worried.	He was	thinking about the landslide.
The children were		They were	

Was Brenda studying from 12 to 12:45?	No, she was having lunch.
Were you living in New York in 1984?	Yes, I was.
	No, I wasn't.

I was walking		
he was walking	*was*	+ V-*ing*
they were walking	*were*	

was not	→	**wasn't**
were not		**weren't**

A Tell about the story. Give true information.

1 Brenda didn't want to wait. Was she putting on her raincoat and boots?

Yes, she was. She was putting on her raincoat and boots.

2 Ken needed to help Ana. Was he driving to San Francisco?

No, he wasn't. He was driving to Malibu.

3 There might be a landslide. Was Alex thinking about Ana?

4 Brenda and Willy didn't want to stay in the house. Were they waiting for Alex?

5 Largo didn't find the formula. Was he pointing a gun at Ken?

6 There was danger of a landslide. Were the police stopping all cars?

B Look at Brenda and Maria's schedule of classes. These are their Monday classes. Today is Tuesday.

Schedule of Monday Classes

	Brenda	Maria
9:00		
9:45	English	mathematics
10:30	Spanish	French
11:15	geography	English
12 noon	lunch	chemistry
12:45	mathematics	lunch
1:30	typing	computer science
2:15	health	history

● **What were they doing yesterday . . . from 9 to 9:45?**
Brenda was studying English, but Maria wasn't. Maria was studying mathematics.

Ask your classmate, like this:

What were you	studying doing	from _____ to _____?
Where were you	living	in 19____?

C It's noon and the house is a mess. What does Alex ask? Who is responsible for the mess—Brenda or Willy?

Alex looks around and sees . . .

1 a wet bathing suit on the chair
Who was swimming this morning?
Brenda, were you swimming this morning?
2 a dish of ice cream on the fridge
3 a Michael Jackson record on the stereo

4 a box of cereal on the table
5 some movie magazines on the floor
6 a *TV Guide* on the bed
7 some Burger Queen bags on the deck
8 a tennis racquet on the couch

1 *Describe experiences*

When Ana was walking with Alex along the beach, she asked about Mona.
Listen to the conversation. Listen again and write the missing words.

ANA   When did you meet your wife?
ALEX In _____. We were in college.
ANA   Where _____ you _____ then? In Los Angeles?
ALEX No, we were in New York. Mona _____ _____ acting and I was going to Columbia University.
ANA   Did you get _____ when you _____ in school?
ALEX Just after we graduated. We were both pretty _____. Brenda was born a year _____.
ANA   How _____ did you live _____ New York?
ALEX Ten years, _____ 1966 _____ 1976. Then we moved to California. I love it here, but Mona always _____ _____ move back to New York.
ANA   I'm _____ about your divorce, Alex.
ALEX Well, Mona and I are still friends. We just have different lives now.

Role Play: Take the roles of Ana and Alex. Alex asks Ana about her life. Ana doesn't tell the truth.

Start with: When did you come to California?

Ana tells Alex:

1975	—come to California
1975–77	—cashier in a Berkeley store
1977	—move to Florida
1977–80	—secretary in a Miami bank
1980	—move back to California

2 *Report what someone said*

A policeman stopped Brenda. Brenda is telling Maria the story.

BRENDA I was turning left when a policeman stopped me. The sign said *No Left Turn*, but I didn't see it.
MARIA   What did the policeman say?
BRENDA He told me not to turn left.

● **Make conversations about the other signs.**

He	said told me	not to	turn left. park there. drive fast.

14

> **Alex was talking to Ana. Largo was hiding in the kitchen.**

Scene One

🔊 From the kitchen, Largo watched Alex. The seashell was in Alex's hand. Now Largo knew. The formula was in the shell.

Alex was talking to Ana. Quietly, Largo moved behind Alex. Largo raised the hand with the gun in it. Largo's hand was over Alex's head. Before Alex turned around, Largo hit him hard with the heavy gun.

ANA   Alex! Alex! Why did you hurt him? Alex doesn't know about the LILAC project.

LARGO He has the formula, and I want it. Find some rope in the kitchen. We're going to tie him up.

ANA   No, I won't help you.

LARGO Yes, you will, or your friend Alex is a dead man.

ANA   Please, please don't hurt Alex. I'll get the rope. Anything you say. But don't hurt Alex.

Questions

1 Where was Largo hiding?
2 What was Ana doing?
3 Who hit Alex? How?
4 Where was the rope?
5 Did Ana help Largo? Why?

Brenda, look!
Dad's hurt.

Scene Two

Brenda and Willy were outside Ana's house. They were watching from the window. First, their father was talking to Ana. Then, a big man came from the kitchen and hit their father over the head. Now Ana was tying their father with a rope.

WILLY Brenda, look! Dad's hurt. They're taking him to the bedroom. He's all tied up.

BRENDA Quiet, Willy. Shh. They might hear us.

WILLY Look. That man is taking Ana outside. They're walking to the deck below.

BRENDA Ana is a spy. I'm sure the big man is Ana's partner. Willy, climb in the bedroom window and untie Dad. I'm going to follow Ana and that man.

WILLY Brenda, don't go! He has a gun. Brenda, wait.

Questions

1 What were Brenda and Willy doing?
2 Who tied Alex?
3 Where did Brenda tell Willy to go?
4 What did Brenda tell Willy to do?
5 What is Brenda going to do?

Speechwork

1 Why *did you* hurt him? [dɪdžə]
2 I won't *help you.* [hɛlpyə]
3 *Anything you say.* [ɛniyəɪŋyəsey]

Police Report

Three men robbed a bank today.

What did they look like?
What were they wearing?

 Tell about the robbers, like this:

One witness said:

"One of the men was bald and had a beard. He was about medium height and average weight. He was wearing striped pants and a white shirt. Oh, and he was wearing sunglasses. He wasn't wearing a hat."

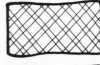 plaid

 striped

 polka dot

 The police found these clues at the Paris Café. Complete the police report. Write a description of the robber:

Clues:

cigarette on the floor
blond curly hair in the carpet
threads of red wool
wrapper from a candy bar
footprint of a running shoe
large brown button
empty can of diet soda
black, leather glove

POLICE REPORT   Date _____

Incident _____

Stolen _____

Description of robber _____

_____

_____

_____

_____

_____

_____

The San Francisco Earthquake: 1906

It was five o'clock in the morning on Wednesday, April 18, 1906. In North Beach, some people were playing cards, dancing, and drinking. But the other parts of the city were quiet. The rich people on Nob Hill were sleeping too. Over 340,000 people lived in San Francisco in 1906.

At twelve minutes after five, the city of San Francisco started to move. Tall buildings came down with a loud crash. Houses were cut in half and people in their beds flew out of broken windows. The expensive houses on Nob Hill were in pieces too. The earthquake was over in a minute.

For three days, San Francisco burned. There were 52 fires in all parts of the city. When the terrible time was over, 500 people were killed and over 300,000 didn't have a home. But the people of San Francisco built their city again. Today about one million people live in this great city.

Thinkabout

	True	False		True	False
1 The people in North Beach were asleep at 5 A.M.	_____	_____	3 There was a terrible fire after the earthquake.	_____	_____
2 People with a lot of money live on Nob Hill.	_____	_____	4 About 340,000 people live in San Francisco today.	_____	_____

Talkabout

What should you do in an emergency?

1 You are in your bed. There's an earthquake. Do you. . . ?
  a run out of the house
  b go under the bed
  c _____

2 You are on the fifth floor of a modern building. There's a terrible fire on the fourth floor. Do you. . . ?
  a jump out of the window
  b take the elevator down
  c _____

3 You are in a car and driving very fast down a hill. The car won't stop because it doesn't have any brakes. Do you. . . ?
  a jump out of the car
  b step on the gas
  c _____

The storm is worse. If the rain doesn't stop, there'll be a landslide.

Dad, look down there. On the lower deck.

Scene One

Ken Matthews was worried. The rain was coming down harder than before. Ken turned the corner. He saw a car on the side of the road. It was Largo's tan Buick.

Quickly, Ken ran down the wooden steps to the house below. Some of the steps were missing. They were washed away by the heavy rain.

Ken opened the door. He heard a noise from the bedroom.

WILLY Dad, Dad. It's Willy. Wake up.
ALEX   Oh . . . Who hit me? Oh, my head. It hurts.
KEN   Where's Ana? I'm Matthews. U.S. agent.
WILLY Ana went with that man.
ALEX   Where did they go, Willy?
WILLY Dad, I don't know. Brenda ran after them.
KEN   Who's Brenda?
ALEX   My daughter.
WILLY Dad, the man has a gun. I saw him.
KEN   C'mon. We've got to find them.

Questions

1 Was the weather getting worse?
2 Where was the tan Buick?
3 What was happening in the bedroom?
4 Why did Alex's head hurt?
5 Who followed Ana and Largo?

Scene Two

📼 Quickly, Ken untied the ropes around Alex. Then the men ran outside. Willy was right behind them.

Alex looked around him. Some of the trees were already broken and sliding down the side of the hill. In a few minutes, the whole hill might fall into the ocean.

ALEX   We have to hurry. If there's a landslide, the whole hill will slide into the ocean.
KEN   Do you see Ana and Brenda?
ALEX   No, the rain is too heavy. It's too dark.
WILLY Dad, look down there. On the lower deck.
KEN   It's Largo. He's pointing a gun at Ana.
ALEX   Oh, my God. Brenda is there too. She's right behind him, but he can't see her.
KEN   Hurry. If we don't stop Largo, he'll kill Ana.

Questions

1 Who untied the ropes?
2 What did Alex see around him?
3 What might happen to the hill?
4 Where's Ana?
5 What might happen to her?

Speechwork

1 If the rain doesn't stop, there'll be a landslide.

2 If we don't stop Largo, he'll kill Ana.

59

The First Conditional—Present Real

It might rain. If it	rains,	I'll go to	a movie.
	doesn't rain,		the beach.
If I don't go to the	supermarket,	I won't have	any milk.
	drugstore,		any aspirin.

If Ken and Alex can't stop Largo, Largo will kill Ana.

If . . .	*Present Simple* ,	I you he we they	will won't	+ *Verb Base*

A Brenda is asking Maria about her weekend plans.

BRENDA What are you going to do this weekend?

MARIA I'm not sure. I might work. What about you?

BRENDA I don't know. If the weather's good, I'll go to the beach. If it rains, I'll watch TV.

● **Ask your classmate, like this:**
What are you going to do this weekend?

If the weather is | good | bad | *,*

I'll _____.

B What are some of the things Brenda has to do today?

● **Tell about Brenda, like this:**

If Brenda washes clothes,
she'll have a clean blouse.

If Brenda doesn't wash clothes,
she won't have a clean blouse.

Brenda has to . . .	Brenda needs . . .
wash clothes	a clean blouse
go to the post office	stamps
go to the supermarket	bread
cook dinner	a hot meal
go to the bank	cash
do her homework	good grades

● **Tell about things you have to do.**

C Ken can't see well because it's raining hard.

If Ken can't see the house, he'll look for Largo's tan Buick.

What will you do. . . . ?

1 if you can't find your pen
If I can't find my pen, I'll borrow . . .
2 if you can't find your house keys
If I can't find my house keys, I'll call . . .
3 find your wallet
4 remember a phone number
5 do your homework
6 spell a word
7 fix your car
8 accept an invitation

1 Request a favor

Maria can't go shopping today because she has to work.
She's asking Brenda to shop for her.

Listen to the conversation. Listen again and write the missing words.

MARIA   Can you do me a favor, Brenda?

BRENDA   Sure.

MARIA   If you go to Dade's, _____ _____ buy a lipstick for me?

BRENDA   Okay. I _____ _____ _____ Dade's anyway. What kind do you want?

MARIA   A _____ red color.

BRENDA   Anything else?

MARIA   Well, _____ _____ _____ to the drugstore, will you get a bottle of aspirin for me?

BRENDA   Do you want one _____ tablets?

MARIA   Fine. Oh, _____ _____ home at five if you want to come over to my house later.

BRENDA   I'm sorry, I _____. If I go to your house, I _____ have time to wash _____.

MARIA   That's okay. I'll come over to your house tomorrow.

Role Play: You can't go to the supermarket or to the drugstore because you have to study. Ask your classmate to shop for you.

Start with: Can you do me a favor? If you go to _____, will you buy _____ for me?

2 Make predictions

Bill has a lot of bills to pay this month:

ELVIRA   When is your electric bill due?

BILL   On the twenty-first.

ELVIRA   Well, if you don't pay the bill, the electric company will shut off your electricity.

● **Make conversations about the other bills.**

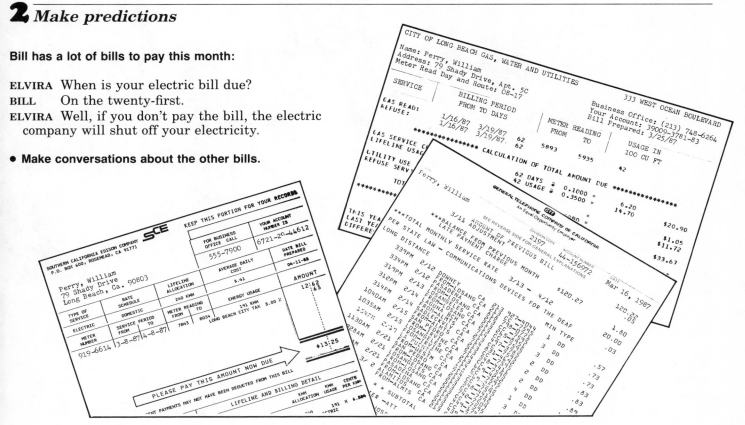

Largo is pointing his gun at Ana. If Ana doesn't jump, Largo will kill her.

If I don't kill you, you'll tell the police about me.

Scene One

🔈 Ana was with Largo on the lower deck. The wind was blowing hard. The man was shouting at Ana. Brenda was behind Largo, but she couldn't hear them. She moved closer.

LARGO Go over there. Against the railing.

ANA I can't. The deck is slippery. It's covered with water.

LARGO If you don't move, I'll use this gun.

ANA What are you going to do to me?

LARGO You're going to have an accident, Dr. Cruz. Don't you know? You shouldn't be out on a night like this.

ANA Please, don't kill me. You have the formula. What do you want with me?

LARGO I want you to jump, Dr. Cruz. When this storm is over, the police will find your body in the ocean.

ANA No, no! I don't want to die.

Questions

1 Where was Ana?
2 Who was shouting?
3 Did Brenda hear them? Why not?
4 What will happen to Ana if she doesn't move?
5 Does Largo want Ana to jump? Why?

Scene Two

Brenda didn't understand. Ana was standing next to the railing and the man wanted to kill her. Maybe Ana wasn't a spy.

Suddenly Ana looked over Largo's shoulder. She saw Brenda! Brenda was behind Largo! Ana looked at Largo. The shell was in Largo's hand. In his other hand, he held the gun.

LARGO Over the railing, Dr. Cruz. Jump!

ANA No, I won't do it. I won't.

LARGO You're going to die, Dr. Cruz. If I don't kill you, you'll tell the police about me.

ANA Please, you have the formula. I won't tell the police. I won't. Please, let me go.

LARGO I'm not a fool. No, you have to die. You know who I am. I'm going to count to three. If you don't jump, Dr. Cruz, I'll shoot you. One. . .

Questions

1 Who was standing next to the railing?
2 Where was Brenda?
3 Did Ana have a gun? Who did?
4 Who had the LILAC formula?
5 Why does Ana have to die?

Speechwork

1 I don't *want to* die. [wɔnə]
2 I *want you to* jump. [wɔntšətə]

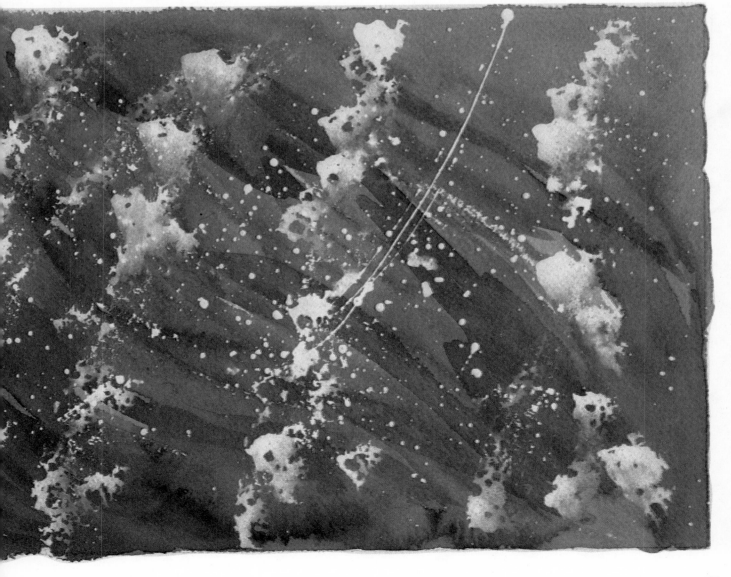

Services

A You are on the corner of Ocean Drive and Canyon Road. Get information and directions, like this:

Excuse me. Where can I fill a prescription?

If you go down Canyon Road, you'll see a drugstore on your right, between the bank and the jeweler's. It's opposite the travel agency.

You also need to....

cash a check	find a newspaper
get a bus	buy a watch
buy a plane ticket	get cough medicine
do a wash	find a doctor
get a cup of coffee	buy fresh fruit

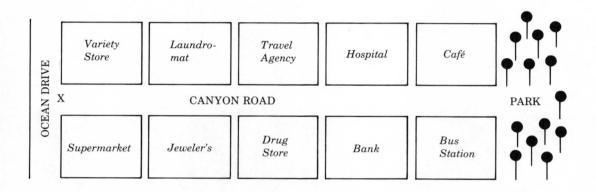

	Variety Store	Laundro-mat	Travel Agency	Hospital	Café
OCEAN DRIVE	X	CANYON ROAD			PARK
	Supermarket	Jeweler's	Drug Store	Bank	Bus Station

B Compare services in this city with services in your country.

If you want to | get a driver's license, <br> fix your car, <br> send a registered letter, | what should you do?

Is it | easier <br> more difficult <br> cheaper <br> more expensive | to do these things in your country?

C Write a letter to a friend. Your friend might visit you in this city. Tell about things to expect:

Dear _____,
If you come to _____, you'll find many things (easier/more difficult) here. If you want to fix your car, you'll have to _____. If you want to send a registered letter, you'll have to _____. If you want to buy...

Hearabout   *Give directions to your house.*

Bill is going to visit Elvira. Elvira is giving directions to Bill.

Listen to the conversation. Draw a line on the map to show the way to Elvira's house. Start at the bus stop.

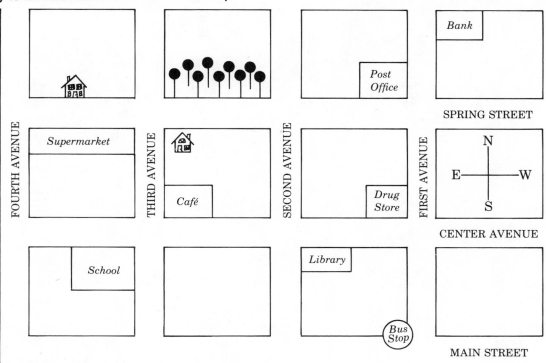

Speakabout

Your friend is visiting your house for the first time. Give directions to take a bus or subway. Tell how to get to your house.

Cues:	You	Your friend	Cues:
		Ask about public transportation.	What bus/subway do I take? Do I take the number _____ bus/subway?
Take the _____ bus and get off at _____.	Give information.		
		Ask for directions.	Where do I walk? How do I get to your house?
Go north/south/east/west on _____ street, then _____. My house is between _____ and _____. It's opposite _____.	Give directions to your house.		

Ana was standing next to the railing. Largo held on to the shell.

Brenda, push.
Push him now!

Scene One

🔊 Ana looked down from the deck. She was frightened. The water was crashing against the big rocks.

Ana felt the railing behind her. It was loose from the heavy rains. The railing was weak. It might break easily. Ana looked at Brenda. Brenda saw the loose railing too. Brenda was behind Largo. Largo was counting to three.

LARGO   . . . two . . . this is your last chance, Dr. Cruz. Jump, or I'll shoot you.

ANA   Brenda, push. Push him now!

BRENDA . . . three!

LARGO   What? The railing. The railing! It's breaking! Help . . . Ah!

ANA   Oh, my God! Largo fell on the rocks! He's dead!

BRENDA Ana, don't move or you'll fall too.

ANA   He dropped the shell on the deck. It's going to fall into the ocean! I've got to get the shell.

BRENDA Ana, don't try. Please! The deck is too slippery. If you move, you'll fall off the deck!

ANA   I'm almost there, Brenda. One more step. There. I've got the shell.

BRENDA Ana, wait. Oh, no! The deck is shaking. Ana, the deck is coming loose!

ANA   Brenda! Help me. Give me your hand. I'm falling. I can't hold on!

Questions

1 Who was frightened? Why?
2 Was the railing loose? Why?
3 Who pushed Largo?
4 What happened to Largo?
5 If Brenda doesn't help, what will happen to Ana?

Scene Two

📼 Brenda reached out and caught Ana's hand. Ana slipped on the wet deck. Her legs were hanging over the side, but Ana held on to Brenda with one hand. In her other hand, Ana held the shell.

BRENDA Ana, please! Please let go of the shell. Take my other hand.

ANA I can't, Brenda. I can't lose the formula now!

BRENDA Ana, please. I can't hold on to you much longer. Drop the shell! You'll fall if you don't drop the shell. Please help me, Ana.

ANA There. I dropped it. Brenda, give me your other hand.

BRENDA Ana, lift up your leg. Put it over the deck. I'll pull you up.

ANA We made it! Oh, Brenda. You saved my life. We're alive!

BRENDA Wait. Oh, no! The deck is shaking again. Ana, the deck is coming loose. I can feel it. We're going to fall into the ocean!

Lift up your leg.
Put it over the deck.

Questions

1 Who caught Ana's hand?
2 Where was Ana?
3 Who had the LILAC formula?
4 Who pulled Ana up?
5 If the deck comes loose, what will happen?

Speechwork

1 Largo held on to the shell.

2 Lift up your leg.

Two-word Verbs

Ana might fall off. She was holding onto Brenda's hand.			
Clean up your room. I cleaned	the room it	up this morning.	

Who does	she he	look like?	Brenda Willy	looks like	her mother. his father.

Separable
clean up ↔ clean *it* up
turn off   turn *them* off

Inseparable
look like *her*
take after *him*

A Tell about the story. Choose from the list to complete the sentences.

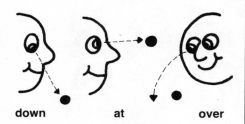

down   **at**   **over**

1 Ana looked _____ Largo. She was frightened.
2 Largo didn't look _____ his shoulder. He didn't see Brenda.
3 Ana looked _____. The ocean was dark and ugly.

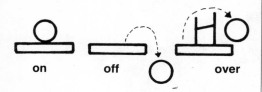

on   **off**   **over**

1 Ana didn't want to jump _____ the deck.
2 Ana and Brenda are standing _____ the lower deck.
3 Ana might fall _____ the railing.

B You can separate these verb parts. Tell what you usually do, then ask your classmate.

At school

1 Do you *look up* words in the dictionary?

I | always
usually
sometimes
never | *look* them *up.*

2 Do you *hand in* your homework on time?
3 Do you *write down* new words?
4 Do you *make up* sentences with new words?
5 Do you *throw away* old homework and tests?

At home

1 Do you *clean up* your room, or does someone else *clean* it *up*?
2 Do you *turn off* the lights, or does someone else *turn* them *off*?
3 Do you *hang up* your clothes, or does someone else *hang* them *up*?
4 Do you *take out* the garbage, or does someone else *take* it *out*?
5 Do you *pick up* dirty dishes, or does someone else *pick* them *up*?

C You cannot separate these verb parts:

Brenda has a strong personality. Brenda *takes after* her mother. She's an independent person. Brenda *looks like* her mother too. They have the same blond hair. Brenda and her mother are good friends, but Brenda doesn't *get along with* her brother. Brenda *is looking forward to* summer vacation. She can't *get into* school. She likes the beach and fast cars.

1 Who do you *look like*—your mother or your father?
2 Who do you *get along with*—your sister(s) or your brother(s)?
3 What are you *looking forward to*—a vacation, a party, a concert?
4 What do you *get into*—sports, cars, music?

1 *Make a judgment*

Brenda and Maria are at the art museum. They're looking at modern paintings. Brenda likes modern art, but Maria doesn't.
Listen to the conversation. Listen again and write the missing words.

BRENDA Look at that painting, the one on the left.
MARIA It's strange. I'm _____ _____ I like it. What do you _____ _____ it?
BRENDA Well, I like it a lot. It's a happy painting. It _____ _____ a flower to me.
MARIA Gee, I don't know. It looks like an _____ painting to me.
BRENDA Oh, I don't think so. I feel happy when I _____ _____ it.

MARIA Maybe you're right. I just can't _____ _____ modern art. I'm more interested in traditional art.
BRENDA Yeah, you like paintings about real people and places.

Role Play: Look at the other painting. Discuss the painting:

1 What do you think about it?
2 What does it look like?
3 How do you feel when you look at it?

Start with: What do you think about that painting?

2 *Give indirect commands*

Alex is telling Brenda to do some chores.

Make conversations, like this:

ALEX Don't forget to *drop off* the dirty shirts at the cleaner's.
BRENDA I won't forget to *drop* them *off*.
ALEX I'd like you to *pick up* the clean shirts too.
BRENDA Okay. I'll *pick* them *up*.

	To drop off . . .	To pick up . . .
Cleaner's	the dirty shirts	the clean shirts
Post Office	the letters	some stamps
Supermarket	the empty bottles	some Coke
Drugstore	the prescription	the pills

The deck is falling apart. It's going to fall into the ocean.

Take this rope. Tie it around your waist.

Scene One

Alex, Willy and Ken watched from the deck above. Largo was dead. Brenda was pulling Ana up onto the deck.

WILLY Dad, look! The lower deck is cracked.

ALEX My God! The deck is breaking apart!

WILLY It's going to fall into the ocean!

KEN Where are the steps to the lower deck?

ALEX They're on the side of the house. Hurry.

WILLY Dad, the steps aren't here. They floated away. How are we going to help Brenda and Ana now?

KEN Willy, get the rope in the bedroom. Alex, tie the rope around me and lower me down to the deck. We've got to reach them before it's too late.

Questions

1 Where were Alex, Willy and Ken?
2 Who fell into the ocean?
3 Who might fall off the deck?
4 What happened to the steps?
5 Who needs the rope? Why?

Scene Two

📼 Alex took the rope and tied it to the door. Then he tied the other end of the rope around Ken. Slowly, Alex and Willy lowered Ken down the side of the hill.

Below, Ken saw Ana and Brenda. They were kneeling on the cracked deck. It was starting to break apart. Ana looked up. She saw Ken. He was hanging from the rope.

ANA   Ken! Help us!
BRENDA   The deck is loose. Hurry!
KEN   Try to move closer to me, Ana. Go slowly.
ANA   Hold on to me, Brenda. Hold tight. I'm almost near Ken.
KEN   Just a few more feet, Ana. Good. Take this rope. Tie it around your waist. Brenda, you too.
BRENDA   The deck! It's moving. It's too late. We're not going to make it!

Questions

1 Where did Alex tie the rope?
2 Who's going to get the women?
3 Where were Brenda and Ana?
4 What did Ana and Brenda do with the rope?
5 Will Ken save the women?

Speechwork

1 the *lower* deck [lowɚ]
2 the *other* end [əðɚ]
3 move *closer* [klowsɚ]

Sizes

What's your American size? Who else wears your
size?

A   Ask about sizes, like this:

	Ana's size	Alex's size
coat	10	42
blouse/shirt	34	16
shoes	8	9½

Can you wear | Ana's / Alex's | coat / shirt / shoes | ?

Is it / Are they | too small / too big | for you?

B   Ask about clothes, like this:

I'd like to try on a/some _____.
Do you wear size _____?
Yes, that's right.
or
No, that's too small/big for me.
I wear size _____.

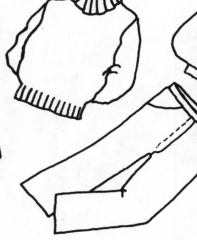

men

SUITS, SWEATERS AND OVERCOATS _____

American and British:	34	36	38	40	42	44	46	48
European:	44	46	48	50	52	54	56	58

SHIRTS _____

American and British:	14	14½	15	15½	16	16½	17	17½
European:	36	37	38	39	40	41	42	43

SHOES _____

American:		7	7½	8	8½	9	9½	10	10½	11	11½
British:	6½	7	7½	8	8½	9	9½	10	10½	11	
European:	39	40	41	42	43	43	44	44	45	45	

women

DRESSES, SUITS AND COATS _____

American:		8	10	12	14	16	18
British:		30	32	34	36	38	40
European:		36	38	40	42	44	46

BLOUSES AND SWEATERS _____

American:		32	34	36	38	40	42	44
British:		34	36	38	40	42	44	46
European:		40	42	44	46	48	50	52

SHOES _____

American:	5	5½	6	6½	7	7½	8	8½	9
British:	3½	4	4½	5	5½	6	6½	7	7½
European:	35	35	36	37	38	38	38½	39	40

C   Your favorite suit, dress or sweater is at the cleaner's. Borrow what you need.

Can I borrow / Would you lend me | your _____?   I wear size _____.
Sure, I have a (color) _____. It should fit you. Try it on.
or
Sorry, my _____ is too big/small for you. I wear size _____.

Californians!

Ethnic Groups

One out of three Californians comes from a minority group. Many Mexican-Americans live in or around Los Angeles. In fact, only one city in the world has a larger Mexican population, and that's Mexico City! Today, southern California life, from food to shopping, housing and entertainment, is all part of Hispanic traditions.

Over 10 percent of California's population is Asian. Beginning in 1850, the Chinese came to Los Angeles and San Francisco. They worked in the gold mines and built the new railroads. Japanese workers came too. As farmers, they changed much of the California desert areas into great farmlands.

The Sun Worshippers

Californians love the sun. They get up early and run a few miles, then go to the beach. That's where the action is. You might see surfers sitting on their cars and looking over the ocean. Don't worry. They're not looking for *Jaws*. They're just waiting for the perfect wave.

The Rich and Famous

You know the "beautiful people"—their faces are on TV screens and in movies. They work in the studios of Hollywood, but they live in the expensive homes of Beverly Hills. You can take a guided tour of the stars' houses. But you won't find Joan Collins in the kitchen!

Thinkabout

	True	False		True	False
1 One out of five Californians is Asian.		✓	3 Movies are made in Hollywood.		
2 Hispanic traditions aren't important in California.			4 Californians spend a lot of time outdoors.		

Writeabout

Write a letter to a friend in another city or country. Tell about the people in this city.

Are there many ethnic groups?
Do people enjoy the outdoors? play sports?

Start with: There are/aren't a lot of different kinds of people in _____.

19 LANDSLIDE

Alex and Willy held on to the rope. Ken was hanging from the other end.

*Dad, look!
What is it?
What's that noise?*

Scene One

Alex and Willy couldn't hold on to the rope much longer. Their arms were aching. Ken was hanging from the other end of the rope. Brenda and Ana were tied to the rope too. Suddenly, Alex and Willy heard a loud noise from above.

WILLY Dad, look! What is it? What's that noise?

ALEX What? Thank God! It's the police rescue helicopter. We've got a chance now.

WILLY Dad, look! The lower deck is moving. It's going to fall into the ocean.

ALEX Hang on tight, Willy. The police are here now. They're helping Ken.

WILLY Dad, I can't see Brenda or Ana!

ALEX Hold the rope, Willy. It's the only way we can save them.

Questions

1 Did Alex's and Willy's arms hurt? Why?
2 Who was hanging from the rope?
3 What was making the loud noise?
4 What might happen to the lower deck?
5 Who was helping Ken?

Scene Two

📼 The police had to hurry. The deck was breaking loose from the hill. The police helicopter was over the cracked deck. A policeman was coming down from the helicopter on a heavy wire. He was carrying other wires with large hooks.

KEN	Here! We're down here!
POLICEMAN	I see you! Grab this hook. I'll get the women.
ANA	Hurry! We can't hold on much longer.
POLICEMAN	Take my hand! I'm putting these belts around you. Then the hooks. We're going to lift you into the helicopter.
BRENDA	I'm ready!
ANA	Me too.
POLICEMAN	Okay! Pull us up! Pull us up now!

Questions

1 Who was coming down from the helicopter?
2 What was he carrying?
3 Who took the hook from the policeman?
4 Where did the policeman put the belts?
5 Who pulled the women up?

Speechwork

1 It's the only way we can *save them*. [seyvəm]
2 He put the belts *around them*. [ərawndəm]

Integration

If Elvira takes the new job, she'll work	at a higher salary. longer hours.

Alex was at Elaine's. He was having lunch from twelve to two.	

If I have to	put in lights, put up shelves,	I'll call	an electrician. a carpenter.

A Elvira is a guard at the Berkeley Science Lab. She might apply for a job as a supervisor. She is comparing jobs.

Old Job	New Job
$15,000/ year	$18,000/ year
35 hours/ week	40 hours/ week
uniforms	no uniforms

● **Tell about the jobs with adjective comparatives:**

1 The new job has a (high) salary.
2 The new job requires (long) hours.
3 The new job gives her (short) vacations.
4 Clothes for the new job will be (expensive).
5 The new job is (responsible) than the old job.

● **What's more important to you?**

1 shorter work hours or higher salary?
2 more responsibility or longer vacations?

B Alex was in New York City last month. He was busy all day Monday.

● **Ask about Alex's day, like this:**

1 What did Alex do at (9) o'clock?
2 What was Alex doing from (10 to 11)?

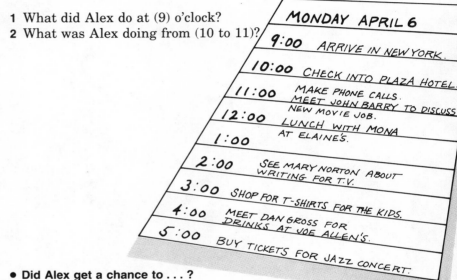

MONDAY APRIL 6
9:00 ARRIVE IN NEW YORK.
10:00 CHECK INTO PLAZA HOTEL.
11:00 MAKE PHONE CALLS. MEET JOHN BARRY TO DISCUSS NEW MOVIE JOB.
12:00 LUNCH WITH MONA AT ELAINE'S.
1:00
2:00 SEE MARY NORTON ABOUT WRITING FOR T.V.
3:00 SHOP FOR T-SHIRTS FOR THE KIDS.
4:00 MEET DAN GROSS FOR DRINKS AT JOE ALLEN'S.
5:00 BUY TICKETS FOR JAZZ CONCERT.

● **Did Alex get a chance to . . . ?**

1 call up some of his friends
2 pick up concert tickets
3 talk about work on a film
4 look for presents

C Alex's house needs some repairs. Look at the Home Services Guide. Who should Alex call?

● **Alex wants to:**

1 put brighter lights in the living room
2 put a lighter coat of paint on the bathroom walls
3 put up wider shelves in the kitchen
4 put up more colorful wallpaper in the bedroom

HOME SERVICES GUIDE

PAINTING/WALLPAPER HANGING—Over 20 years experience. Very clean work. Bill 763-3954

HOME IMPROVEMENT—Plumbing. Electrical. Carpentry. All work guaranteed. Judy & Carol 274-8442.

REPAIRS—TV, STEREO, STOVE, REFRIGERATOR. No job too big or too small. Dan 479-3331.

● **Alex needs someone to look at:**

1 a broken washing machine
2 a leaky pipe in the bathroom
3 a broken television
4 a cracked kitchen table

● **Can you do these jobs yourself? If you can't, who will you call?**

1 *Make an exchange*

Last week, Maria bought a radio from Dan's Discount Mart, and now it isn't working. She's trying to get her money back from the salesclerk.
Listen to the conversation. Listen again and write the missing words.

CLERK What can I do for you, miss?
MARIA I want to return this radio. I _____ it here last week.
CLERK Let me take a _____ _____ it.
MARIA I _____ it _____ this morning. It _____ _____ a funny noise, then it stopped.
CLERK Well, it doesn't seem to work.
MARIA Of course it doesn't work. It's _____. And _____ like to get my money _____, please. I paid $_____ for that radio. Here's the receipt.
CLERK I'm _____, but we don't give refunds.
MARIA If you don't refund my money, _____ _____ to the police.
CLERK Oh, that _____ _____ necessary. Let me give you a new radio.
MARIA Fine, but turn it on first. I want to make sure it works.

Role Play: The tape recorder is broken. Return it and ask for a refund.

2 *Discuss alternatives*

It's 10 P.M. and Elvira and Bill want to have a snack. Talk about two restaurants in this city, like this:

BILL   Let's go to Tony's Bar & Grill.
ELVIRA It's too noisy there. What about Café Paris? It's a quieter place.
BILL   Tony's is closer. It's around the corner.
ELVIRA But the food at the Café Paris is better.
BILL   Yeah, but it's more expensive than Tony's.

Tony's Bar & Grill

Live Rock 'n' Roll Music
Pitcher of beer $4.00

Minimum $5.00 per person   Piano music nightly

Everyone was safe in the police helicopter. Ana had to think about the future.

Scene One

🔊 The policeman helped Ana and Brenda into the helicopter. They brought Ken up next.

In a few minutes, the helicopter was over the house. The policeman went down with the wires and hooks to get Alex and Willy.

In the helicopter, Alex took the heavy belt off Willy.

WILLY   Dad, look at Ana's house!
ANA   The house! It's moving!
BRENDA   There it goes. Right into the ocean.
WILLY   Dad, what about *our* house?
ALEX   Look over there. It's still standing. I built that house. It's never going to fall into the ocean.
KEN   Are you people okay? Ana, it's over. Largo won't hurt you now.
ANA   Oh, Ken. I lost the formula. It's in the ocean.
BRENDA   Yeah, Largo got the formula after all!
ALEX   Brenda, we don't need your bad jokes now.
BRENDA   Well, I know what I need. Officer, do you have any chocolate ice cream on this helicopter?

Questions

1 Who rescued Alex and Willy?
2 What happened to Ana's house?
3 Is Alex's house all right? Why?
4 Is Ana upset? Why?
5 Who made a joke?

We'd love to have
you stay, Ana.

Scene Two

📼 The next day, the sun was shining. It was a beautiful day in southern California. Ana went back to the house with Alex and the children.

There were broken trees and mud everywhere. Pieces of wood and furniture from Ana's house were all over the beach.

ANA   What a mess!

ALEX   Yeah, it looks like Brenda's room.

BRENDA C'mon, Dad. I'm not *that* messy.

ALEX   Ana, what are you going to do now?

ANA   Well, I'm not sure. I don't want to go back to that laboratory. Maybe I should take a vacation.

WILLY   Stay with us, Ana. Dad, can't Ana stay with us for a while?

ALEX   We'd love to have you stay, Ana. Really. It is usually quiet here, you know.

WILLY   Dad, are you kidding?

ANA   But I don't have a bathing suit with me!

BRENDA Well, I have this red bathing suit . . .

WILLY   Oh, Brenda!

Questions

1 What was the weather like?
2 What did they see on the beach?
3 Is Ana going back to her job at the laboratory?
4 Who should take a vacation?
5 Will Ana accept Alex's invitation?

Speechwork

1 What about our house?

2 I'm not that messy.

Entertainment

What's going on this weekend? Are there any good plays or concerts? What's happening in sports?

A **Ask about the weekend events, like this:**

If you go to a theater,

where will you go?
how much will you spend?
what time will you get there?
which tickets will you buy—the cheaper or more expensive ones?

	FRIDAY	SATURDAY	SUNDAY
Theaters	**The Real Thing—** "Tragic story of love and selfishness." GOLDEN THEATER 8 P.M. $30, $40 tickets	**Cats**—"The musical spectacular!" Seats $28, $35, $45 BOOTH THEATER 2 P.M., 8 P.M.	**Noises Off!**— "A very funny British comedy . . ." WEST SIDE THEATER 7:30 P.M. Seats $25, $35
Concerts	**MALIBU JAZZ FESTIVAL** Kanakawa—Japanese Jazz group All seats $6. 7 P.M.	**MOZART** at the **HOLLYWOOD BOWL** Pinchas Zuckerman, violin, and Marc Neikrug, piano. 9 P.M. $15, $25 tickets	**OPERA IN ORANGE PARK** *Carmen* with Victoria Vergara and Robert Hale Free admission 6 P.M.
Sporting Events	**BASEBALL** San Francisco Giants vs San Diego Padres Jack Murphy Stadium Tickets $8, $10 8 P.M.	**SOCCER** L.A. Strikers vs N.Y. Cosmos at Los Angeles Seats $10, $15 at 7 P.M.	**AUTOMOBILE RACING** at Southern California Raceway Santa Monica Blvd. at 1 P.M. Admission $4.50

B **Give your opinion. What's. . . ?**

1 more relaxing—a baseball game or an opera performance
2 more boring—a tragic play or an automobile race
3 more interesting—a jazz concert or a soccer game

C **Decide where to go this weekend.**

1 Your mother and father visit you. Where should you take them? Where shouldn't you take them?
2 Your brother is with you today. If together you have only $15, where will you go?
3 You hate the opera. Your girlfriend/boyfriend hates sports. You love to wear bluejeans. She/he loves to wear nice clothes. Can you decide on a place to go?

Hearabout   *Talk about advantages and disadvantages*

Alex and Ana are deciding on a place to go this weekend.
Listen to the conversation. Write the missing information
on the Magic Mountain advertisement.

Dinner Theater
SAT. & SUN. 6 P.M.

My Fair Lady

—musical comedy—

$25 per person

Includes dinner and show

for Reservations
CALL 518-3391

Universal Studios Tour

—See what movies
are made of
—See live TV shows

Located just 3 minutes north
of Hollywood and Vine.

Summer & Holidays 9 A.M.—5 P.M.
$12 Admission with free TV show

Telephone 508-9600 for information

Magic Mountain
Family Amusement Park

Open daily at 10 A.M.

35 Spectacular Rides
America's first 360 degree
roller coaster

$_____ per person

Price includes_____

_____

_____

Only _____ miles from Los Angeles.

Call 277-6198 for information

Speakabout

Choose two events happening in this city, or choose two
of the advertisements. Decide on a place to go this weekend. Talk about the advantages and disadvantages of
each.

Cues:	You	Your friend	Cues:
Where would you like to go? What about _____?	Suggest a place.		
		Tell about advantages. Suggest another place.	If we go to _____, we can _____. The ticket price includes _____.
Well, _____ is more fun (closer).	Talk about advantages/ disadvantages		Okay, but _____ is cheaper (more expensive).
I really want to/don't want to go to _____.	Agree/ disagree.		I think we should/shouldn't go to _____.

Unit 1

MANAGER May I help you, sir?
LARGO I want a room, please. A single room.
MANAGER How long are you going to stay?
LARGO Two or three days.
MANAGER The room is $35 a day. Are you going to pay with cash or a credit card?
LARGO Cash. And I want a room in the back. A quiet one.
MANAGER Number 23. Here's the key. You can park your car in front.
LARGO Fine. And I don't want any visitors.
MANAGER Yes, sir.

Unit 3

MARIA Well, how was the movie? Did you like *Tarzan*?
BRENDA Oh, *that* movie! It was terrible. The acting was lousy. I left early. The action was too slow.
MARIA Didn't you like it at all?
BRENDA No, it was pretty bad.
MARIA What about the new Indiana Jones one?
BRENDA Oh, that was a wonderful movie. I loved it. The story moved very fast and the characters were interesting.
MARIA I guess you really enjoyed the movie.
BRENDA Yeah, it was great.

Unit 5

DOCTOR How are you feeling?
ALEX Lousy. I have a bad pain here, in my stomach.
DOCTOR Hm. Do you have a stomachache now?
ALEX Yeah, and it really hurts.
DOCTOR Tell me, Alex, do you drink six glasses of water every day?
ALEX Well, no, I don't.
DOCTOR You know, you should drink a lot of water. And you should eat fresh fruit.
ALEX I know you're right. But, please, give me some medicine for my stomach.

Unit 7

FIRST MAID We can't go in there. Don't you see the sign?
SECOND MAID But we should clean the room now. We have to clean it every morning.
FIRST MAID Well, we can't now. The sign says *Do Not Disturb*.
SECOND MAID Let's come back this afternoon. We'll clean it then.
FIRST MAID You can, but not me. I won't work late. I have to get home early.
SECOND MAID Room twenty-four is empty. Let's clean that one now.

Unit 9

POLICE Hey, mister. You can't go up that road. It's almost flooded.
KEN I'm a U.S. agent. I have to get to Ocean Beach Drive.
POLICE You shouldn't go. It's dangerous, sir. There might be a landslide.
KEN Did you see a big man with a mustache? He's driving a 1985 tan Buick?
POLICE Yeah, he wanted to get his sister. He said her name was Ana.
KEN I've got to find that man. I'm going to 214 Ocean Beach Drive.
POLICE The rescue helicopter will be here soon. We can take you to the house.
KEN No, I can't wait. When the helicopter arrives, come and get us.

Unit 11

BILL Why do you live in the city? You should move to the country.
ELVIRA I like the city. Life in the city is more exciting. You can go to movies and theaters, and the shopping is better.
BILL Yeah, but it's prettier in the country. There are trees and flowers and the air is cleaner.
ELVIRA That's true, but it isn't very interesting in the country. You know I don't like hiking or fishing.
BILL Well, it is cheaper to live in the country, and it is a lot safer.
ELVIRA No, I won't move. My apartment might be more expensive, but I'm happier in the city.
BILL Don't forget. You can visit me when you want some peace and quiet.

Unit 13

ANA When did you meet your wife?
ALEX In 1967. We were in college.
ANA Where were you living then? In Los Angeles?
ALEX No, we were in New York. Mona was studying acting and I was going to Columbia University.
ANA Did you get married when you were in school?
ALEX Just after we graduated. We were both pretty young. Brenda was born a year later.
ANA How long did you live in New York?
ALEX Ten years, from 1966 to 1976. Then we moved to California. I love it here, but Mona always wanted to move back to New York.
ANA I'm sorry about your divorce, Alex.
ALEX Well, Mona and I are still friends. We just have different lives now.

Unit 15

MARIA Can you do me a favor, Brenda?
BRENDA Sure.
MARIA If you go to Dade's, will you buy a lipstick for me?
BRENDA Okay. I'm going to Dade's anyway. What kind do you want?
MARIA A dark red color.
BRENDA Anything else?
MARIA Well, if you go to the drugstore, will you get a bottle of aspirin for me?

BRENDA Do you want one hundred tablets?
MARIA Fine. Oh, I'll be home at five if you want to come over to my house later.
BRENDA I'm sorry, I can't. If I go to your house, I won't have time to wash my hair.
MARIA That's okay. I'll come over to your house tomorrow.

Unit 17

BRENDA Look at that painting, the one on the left.
MARIA It's strange. I'm not sure I like it. What do you think about it?
BRENDA Well, I like it a lot. It's a happy painting. It looks like a flower to me.
MARIA Gee, I don't know. It looks like an angry painting to me.
BRENDA Oh, I don't think so. I feel happy when I look at it.
MARIA Maybe you're right. I just can't get into modern art. I'm more interested in traditional art.
BRENDA Yeah, you like paintings about real people and places.

Unit 19

CLERK What can I do for you, miss?
MARIA I want to return this radio. I bought it here last week.
CLERK Let me take a look at it.
MARIA I turned it on this morning. It was making a funny noise, then it stopped.
CLERK Well, it doesn't seem to work.
MARIA Of course it doesn't work. It's broken. And I'd like to get my money back, please. I paid $9.97 for that radio. Here's the receipt.
CLERK I'm sorry, but we don't give refunds.
MARIA If you don't refund my money, I'll go to the police.
CLERK Oh, that won't be necessary. Let me give you a new radio.
MARIA Fine, but turn it on first. I want to make sure it works.

Unit 4

ALEX   When did you get this ticket, Brenda?

BRENDA Last week—on the tenth. I parked the car in a "No Parking" area.

ALEX   What time was it?

BRENDA At eleven in the morning. You can't park there before noon. I didn't see the sign.

ALEX   Where were you parked?

BRENDA On Center Avenue, opposite the post office.

ALEX   Well, how much is this ticket going to cost me?

BRENDA Oh, Daddy. The fine is only ten dollars.

ALEX   From now on, Brenda, I want you to follow the rules. No more parking tickets or you can't drive the car.

Unit 8

SUPERVISOR Burger Queen.

BRENDA   I'd like to leave a message for Maria Gomez, please.

SUPERVISOR Who's calling, please?

BRENDA   Brenda Stern. That's S-T-E-R-N.

SUPERVISOR What's the message?

BRENDA   Tell her I've got to go to the library—we planned to go to the beach—so I won't be able to meet her at the beach. But I'll be home at six o'clock.

SUPERVISOR Is there anything else?

BRENDA   Yes, tell her to please call me tonight after dinner.

SUPERVISOR Your telephone number, miss?

BRENDA   My number is 462-1305, and thanks.

Unit 12

PEDRO I'd like to rent a car. For tomorrow. What do you have?

CLERK Well, we have Fords and Buicks, both manual and automatic transmission. The Buicks are more expensive.

PEDRO I'll take the cheaper one. And a car with a manual, please.

CLERK Well, we have a Ford free tomorrow and it's a manual. It's the model with a sunroof. At $25 a day.

PEDRO Fine. I want the car for two days. I'll pick it up at eleven in the morning.

CLERK Okay. That's April sixteenth, with the return on the eighteenth. That'll be $50 for the two days rental and another $10 for the insurance.

PEDRO Is the mileage free?

CLERK Yes, just return the car with a full tank of gas.

Unit 16

ELVIRA Get off the bus on the corner of Main Street and First Avenue. Walk up First Avenue, going north. You'll see Center Avenue. There's a drugstore on the corner.

BILL   Do I go east there?

ELVIRA No, walk north on First Avenue. If you walk up First Avenue, you'll see a post office on the corner. That's Spring Street.

BILL   Do I turn on Spring Street?

ELVIRA Yes, now walk west on Spring Street. Keep walking. You'll come to Second Avenue. You'll see a park on your right.

BILL   Don't you live near the park?

ELVIRA Yes, but you have to cross Third Avenue. My house is between Third and Fourth Avenue, opposite the supermarket.

Unit 20

ALEX Where would you like to go? What about *My Fair Lady*?

ANA   Well, the price of the ticket includes dinner and the show. But I'd like to be outdoors in the sunshine.

ALEX Okay. I guess you don't want to see Universal Studios. It's pretty interesting, but the studios are hot and crowded.

ANA   You know, if we go to Magic Mountain, we can take the kids. Anyway, an amusement park is more fun than a TV show.

ALEX Yeah, Willy should like the roller coaster ride.

ANA   Won't he be frightened?

ALEX Nah, I'll be with him.

ANA   It's cheaper than the studio tour. Tickets to Magic Mountain are only $8 per person and that includes all the rides. And children under 17 get a free T-shirt. The kids will love that. Is Magic Mountain near here?

ALEX It's about 25 miles from Los Angeles. Universal Studios is closer, but the drive to Magic Mountain is nice. I'll let Brenda drive.

ANA   Oh, terrific. If Brenda drives, I'll really be ready for the roller coaster.

1

step	worry	January
rock	follow	February
below	pay for	March
shampoo	park	April
cash	check out	May
electricity	repair	June
laundry	ring/rang	July
cleaner's	leave/left	August
vacancy	quick	September
arrangement	twentieth	October
picnic	twenty-first	November
pick up	thirtieth	December

2

cloth	deluxe	climb
knife	economy	rest
oven	date	carefully
company	take out	wild
polite	fold	island
vacation	dry	How come . . . ?
cabin	push	by foot
sandy	hike	back in a minute
bar	fish	accommodations
boat	sail	air-conditioning
bicycle	sightsee	guided tour
raincoat	eat out	
shorts	get around	

3

curtain	immediately	tie
gun	softly	catch
sunny	rudely	dress
bruise	grade	weigh
face	action	hold/held
joke	character	Take it easy.
patient	interesting	traffic light
quickly	straight	waste time
alive	blonde	pretty good
pound	laugh	miles per hour
tall	jump	
thick	drop	

4

easy	cabinet	vehicle
especially	toxic	fine
maybe	glue	type
care	prescription	remove
sign	metal	find out about
warning	corrosive	worry about
elevator	poisonous	follow a rule
stairway	container	I don't care.
fire	substance	Huh?
speed limit	paint	get married
secretly	violation	

5

anxiously	concert	Would you like...?
sunshine	theater	brush your teeth
real	glass	get a job
can	meal	join the army
package	anytime	save money
frozen	advice	(not) sure
meat	expect	someone else

disappointed	celebrate	get out of here
government	might	happy to see you
spy	should	
graduation	write/wrote	

6

weather	shine	tomato
cloudy	season	pepper
landslide	fall	grape
climate	winter	pear
distance	spring	peach
mild	summer	cherry
dry	beef	a little/a few
giant	chop	What's the matter?
regular	donut	out of (something)
nothing	pie	kilo
more	onion	ounce
each	lettuce	dozen
believe	carrot	loaf
lie	celery	bunch

7

handkerchief	disturb	Don't worry.
mouth	return	Don't forget to. . . .
steak	bore	make a visit
bottle	remind	make plans
needle	When . . . ?	for about an hour
flood	heavy rain	a long line
maid	up the road	

8

public	part	look up (some-thing)
library	reach (a place)	roll of film
reference	read about	passport
copy	I've got (some-thing)	money order
service	I've got to . . .	take a message
available	back room	leave a message
weapon	cash a check	
kid		

9

manager	rescue	feel/felt
several	helicopter	lock
rope	leather	depart
sharp	wool	own
supervisor	cotton	hire
honest	sunglasses	fill
careless	cat	refuse
business	drawer	in danger
receptionist	lost	call in
typist	cut	give permission
almost	ache	

10

announcer	salad	painting
bulletin	beer	collection
take care of	soda	variety
brand new	spinach	condition
quiet	corn	fluent
be able to	beans	auction
appetizer	peas	repeat
main course	roast	shut off

beverage	fried	lose
dessert	boiled	exchange
vegetable	tax	complete
soup	used	employ
melon	art	

11

strong	funny	exciting
step	different	popular
loose	forecast	suburb
sea	partly	flower
mud	average	tree
drawer	windy	life
friendlier	cool	discuss
young	mild	take out
smart	better	turn over
serious	worse	because of
shy	mystery	six feet tall
outgoing	novel	sense of humor
thin	enjoyable	peace and quiet

12

boot	manual	tank
powerful	shift	reserve
economical	convertible	prefer
feature	tape deck	talk about
value	crowded	daily
mileage	reliable	weekly
engine	comfortable	light/dark
transmission	private	some kind of
gallon	model	be in trouble
automatic	full	

13

flashlight	blow	that's all
frightened	point	leave someone
noise	put on	alone
geography	come from	wait for
history	look around	computer science
typing	through	responsible for
mathematics	then	move back to
watch	just	from . . . to

14

partner	footprint	brakes
bald	diet	emergency
beard	glove	earthquakes
robber	height	modern
medium	weight	build/built
average	rob	fly/flew
witness	raise	know/knew
plaid	turn around	hit/hit
polka dot	come down	play cards
striped	untie	step on the gas
thread	crash	cut in half
wrapper	burn	

15

worried	wash away	spell
missing	run after	What about you?
bill	slide	fall/fell
due	borrow	do someone a favor
gas	shut off	do homework
electricity		

16

closer	cover	cough medicine
against	use	registered letter
railing	kill	get a license
slippery	count	fill a prescription
fool	shout	bus station
difficult	cross	laundromat
storm	die	café
shoulder	shoot	jeweler's
jump	keep walking	

17

break/broke	pick up	get into
shake/shook	hand in	someone else
slip	make up	last chance
drop	throw away	take my hand
lift	clean up	save someone's life
hold on (to)	hang up	museum
come loose	take after	be interested in
reach out	get along with	traditional
drop off	look forward to	modern

18

cracked	try on	the other end
tight	kneel/knelt	to make it
waist	borrow	tradition
feet	lend	ethnic
Who else . . . ?	fit	minority
float away	size	percent
break apart	above	farmer
hang from	around	another

19

longer	electrician	break loose
suddenly	carpentry	put in
wire	plumber	put up
hook	receipt	the only way
salary	refund	coat of paint
uniform	necessary	hang wallpaper
responsible	tape recorder	get something
wide	pitcher	back
colorful	minimum	take a look at
plumbing	experience	around the corner
leaky	grab	make sure
pipe	pull up	

20

future	together	stadium
everywhere	opera	theater
wood	musical	raceway
tragic	boring	located
spectacular	admission	take off
violin	include	Are you kidding?
piano	kid	advantage
racing	ride	disadvantage
relaxing	studio	

p	spend, past, hope
b	big, tube, bless
t	still, take, past
d	dig, tide, raised
k	kick, cash, drink
g	get, beg, bigger
č	cheese, pitcher, church
ǰ	judge, jungle, gem
f	phone, foot, life
v	very, cave, live
θ	thing, ether, with
ð	the, either
s	sing, fast, face
z	size, zoo, rise
š	she, chef, mission
ž	pleasure, beige, casual
h	hot, reheat, help
m	moon, summer, some
n	noon, funny, cane
ŋ	finger, singer, sing
r	rare, increase, clear
l	lose, cool, release
w	wet, question, swing
y	yellow
ᴅ	butter, riding
ʔ	kitten, cotton
iy	seat, keep, ski
ɪ	sit, skip, dish
ey	same, pay, eight
ɛ	set, guessed, blessed
æ	sat, grass, dad
ə	some, sum, enough
a	got, farm, possible
uw	suit, zoo, glue
ʊ	soot, put, could
ow	soap, so, grow
ɔ	law, cough, applaud
ay	sight, spy, hide
aw	how, cloud, mouth
ɔy	boy, soil, noise
ɔr	sort, court, war
ɚ	hurt, worse, curl
ḷ	believe, police, bottle
m̩	tomato, bottom
n̩	connect, cotton